D1555985

WENDOVER
01296 623649

3 1 AUG 2007

Please return/renew this item by the last
date shown. Books may also be renewed
by phone and the Internet.

Buckinghamshire
libraryservice
CULTURE AND LEARNING

www.buckscc.gov.uk/libraries

L 28

WENDOVER. TEL. 623649.

Call to Arms 1985
has been published
in a Limited Edition
of which this is

Number

A complete list of the
original subscribers
is printed at the
back of the book

CALL TO ARMS

Richard Simkin's rather dashing print of the Royal Bucks Hussars, published in December 1897. Lord Chesham was responsible for a number of uniform changes in 1892 including the introduction of the closely-braided jacket. The busby had been introduced in 1872/3 although the artillery troop had worn it earlier. (NAM)

The officers of B Company, 1/1st Bucks Battalion in trench kit (including clubs), May 1916. Lt E. N. C. Woollerton and Lt J. Rolleston at the rear, Captain L. W. Crouch and Captain H. V. Combs in the front. Crouch, former Deputy Clerk to Bucks County Council, was killed on 21 July 1916 in a moonlit attack. He was 30. (CRO)

CALL TO ARMS

THE STORY OF
BUCKS' CITIZEN SOLDIERS
FROM THEIR ORIGINS TO DATE

BY

IAN F. W. BECKETT

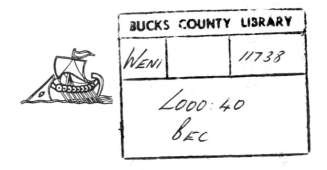

BUCKS COUNTY LIBRARY

WENI | | 11738

L000:40
BEC

BARRACUDA BOOKS LIMITED
BUCKINGHAM, ENGLAND
MCMLXXXV

PUBLISHED BY BARRACUDA BOOKS LIMITED
BUCKINGHAM, ENGLAND
AND PRINTED BY
LEICESTER PRINTERS LIMITED

BOUND BY
HUNTER & FOULIS LIMITED
EDINBURGH, SCOTLAND

JACKET PRINTED BY
CHENEY & SONS LIMITED
BANBURY, OXON

PHOTOLITHOGRAPHY BY
CAMERA GRAPHICS LIMITED
AMERSHAM, ENGLAND

DISPLAY TYPE SET IN BASKERVILLE
AND TEXT SET IN 10½/12pt BASKERVILLE BY
KEY COMPOSITION
NORTHAMPTON, ENGLAND

© Ian F. W. Beckett 1985

All rights reserved. No part of this publication may be reproduced,
stored in a retrieval system, or transmitted, in any form or by any
means, electronic, mechanical, photocopying, recording or
otherwise, without the prior permission of Barracuda Books Limited.

Any copy of this book issued by the Publisher as clothbound or as a
paperback is sold subject to the condition that it shall not by way of
trade or otherwise, be lent, re-sold, hired out or otherwise circulated
without the Publisher's prior consent, in any form of binding or
cover other than that in which it is published, and without a similar
condition including this condition being imposed on a
subsequent purchaser.

ISBN 0 86023 245 X

Contents

Foreword

by Dr John Clarke, University of Buckingham

In Rev Jack Linnell's classic book *Old Oak*, the author describes a scene at the village smithy of Silverstone, on the borders between Northamptonshire and Buckinghamshire, in the crucial year of 1848. As a young boy, Linnell had watched his uncles — with uncharacteristically grim faces — sharpening their sabres on the blacksmith's grindstone before mounting their horses and riding off to Buckingham. From Buckingham they were to go with others from the neighbouring towns and villages and assemble on Hounslow Heath to help the Duke of Wellington meet the expected Chartist-inspired Revolution. It is easy to imagine both the pride and the fears of young Linnell, fears for the safe return for his favourite uncle Tom — 'a famous local cricketer and quoit player, a keen follower of the Grafton, champion swordsman of the Bucks Hussars, bandmaster, choirmaster, Sunday school teacher and at times Churchwarden'. Of course there was no revolution in 1848 — but at least in part that was due to men like Tom Linnell and volunteer regiments like the Bucks Hussars.

Jack Linnell tells his story well and with considerable dramatic effect. But the scene he describes was by no means unique. We learn from *Call to Arms* that similar sabre sharpenings must have taken place in virtually every community in Buckinghamshire. Indeed, 1848 itself was only one of the the many crises in which Buckinghamshire responded to the call. The weapons may have changed over the centuries, but the emotions would have been very much the same.

In this valuable book Ian Beckett tells the story of the 'amateur' soldiers of Buckinghamshire from earliest times to the present. We see them not just in their military aspects but in their social, political and emotional role. The militia, the yeomanry and the volunteers of the nineteenth century formed some of the most important institutions in the life of the county. The wars of this century have shown that 'amateur' soldiers could become brave and competent fighting men in the service of King and Country. Readers of *Call To Arms* will acquire a great deal of information; they will also gain a new pride in the patriotisim and loyalty of men who in many cases were their own forebears.

Publisher's Note:
Coincident with publication of this book, the Buckingham Heritage Trust Limited has been formed as a charitable company to acquire and restore the 18th century Buckingham Gaol and to create therein a Heritage Centre. It is hoped that the presently dispersed Auxiliary Forces Collection, representing surviving relics of the militia, yeomanry and volunteers, will be drawn together by the now also forming Buckinghamshire Military Museum Trust. It is intended to mount a permanent display on behalf of the latter at the Old Gaol Heritage Centre. The author's royalties from this book will be donated to the Buckinghamshire Military Museum Trust.

Introduction

Some years ago I rashly criticised in print the publication of a photographic history of Hertfordshire military units, on the grounds that the considerable amount of material collected by its author, John Sainsbury, should have been used for a full length academic monograph on the amateur military tradition of that county. My view of the necessity for historians to seriously consider the impact of auxiliary military forces on local society has not changed, but I am forced to recognise that, in a difficult economic climate, publishers are unwilling to commit themselves to specialist academic titles of a local content. I am thus both extremely apologetic to John Sainsbury and also very grateful to Barracuda Books in offering this illustrated history of Bucks military units.

In the process, I have taken the opportunity to correct the many errors concerning Bucks units that have continued to appear in accounts of this county's history. There have been a few books on Bucks units, the last of which was published in 1950. None have dealt with the county's military past as comprehensively as this book, although it has been impossible in the space available to do full justice to all the units raised in the county in the past. I have sought, however, to give the essential flavour of each creation and to relate them to the national context of the development of the amateur military tradition in England.

In many respects, this is actually a story of continuity, since the various forces raised, from the Anglo-Saxon fyrd to the Home Guard of 1940, have often performed precisely the same social and military functions. They have been raised both as a counter to threats of invasion, as well as in a constabulary role, and as a wider means of social control through participation and assimilation. They have also provided a supplement to the regular army, if not an alternative, while effectively preventing the raising of a regular army by conscription until 1916. Auxiliaries have, in the process, been far more visible to society as a whole than regular troops and have invariably operated in the full glare of local attention, be it favourable or hostile. There has invariably been a mutual dependence between the auxiliary forces and the society from which they have been recruited, ranging from trade to employment and local politics, while the auxiliaries have represented opportunity to individuals in its widest sense. In short, the auxiliary forces of this and other counties have been an essential point of contact between society and army in England, and involved a wide cross-section in military affairs who would not otherwise have chosen to become so involved. Nothing which consumed so much time and effort in past generations could really fail to be of considerable significance for the historian, and it is to be hoped that far more attention will be devoted to the consequences of the amateur military tradition in this and other counties.

I owe thanks to many people in the preparation of this book, not least to Rev Arthur Taylor of Aylesbury Grammar School, who first introduced me to the military units of Buckinghamshire over twenty years ago. A large number of people have been kind enough to allow me to copy prized photographs in their possession, and my thanks go to Mrs S.

9

Bernard, W. T. Chenery Esq, Mrs Susan Cowdy, R. G. Davies Esq, E. Godfrey Esq, Mrs D. Page, Lord Parmoor, W. G. Pearson Esq, Mrs D. Pitcher, R. Roper Esq, Mrs P. Stevens, Major G. M. I. Stroud, J. Suggers Esq and D. Robinson Esq, Mrs D. H. Tebbutt, Mrs B. M. Turner, Major E. Viney, Mrs P. Waters, Mrs M. White and Ted Hooton Esq for the illustrations they loaned. A large number of documentary sources have also been consulted in the research I have undertaken on Bucks units, and the following are thanked for their kindness in allowing me to consult archives in their possession: the Rt Hon Lord Burnham, Lord Parmoor, Sir Ralph Verney Bt, His Honour Judge L. J. Verney, Colonel John Christie-Miller, Major E. Viney, the Bodleian Library, the British Library, the Huntington Library, the Mass Observation Archive at the University of Sussex, the Public Record Office, N. M. Rothschild Archive, the National Army Museum, the Bucks County Museum and the Imperial War Museum. A number of former members of the Royal Bucks Hussars and the Bucks Battalions have also been kind enough to grant me interviews, namely Colonel C. L. Hanbury, Colonel J. Owen Jones, Captain C. H. Perkins, W. G. Pearson Esq, J. B. Clark Esq, J. Lawrence Esq, S. Lawrence Esq, the late P. E. Pitcher Esq, the late L. Burnham Esq, J. R. R. Stammers Esq, A. Seymour Esq, J. Tranter Esq, R. Francis Esq and Major E. Viney. Assistance in tracing documents or veterans has been rendered by Captain C. O. Pilgrim, A. G. Curtis Esq, and J. E. Pemberton Esq of the University of Buckingham. Thanks are also due to Bob Goodall Esq and R. B. Gibbs Esq for taking the photographs.

Finally, a considerable debt is owed to the staff of the Bucks County Record, especially Hugh Hanley and his predecessor as County Archivist, E. J. Davis. They have given me the utmost assistance in sustaining my obsession with Bucks military units for the past twenty years. However, neither they nor any others mentioned above are responsible for any errors that remain. It has taken a long time to commit this research to print, and I hope that I may be able to offer the full length study I originally set out to write at some future date. I am particularly indebted to all who have subscribed in order that this book could appear.

Royal Military Academy,
Sandhurst,
February 1985

Dedication

For my grandmother, Edith Sarah Beer (née Batson) and
my great aunt, Annie Martha Brown (née Batson).

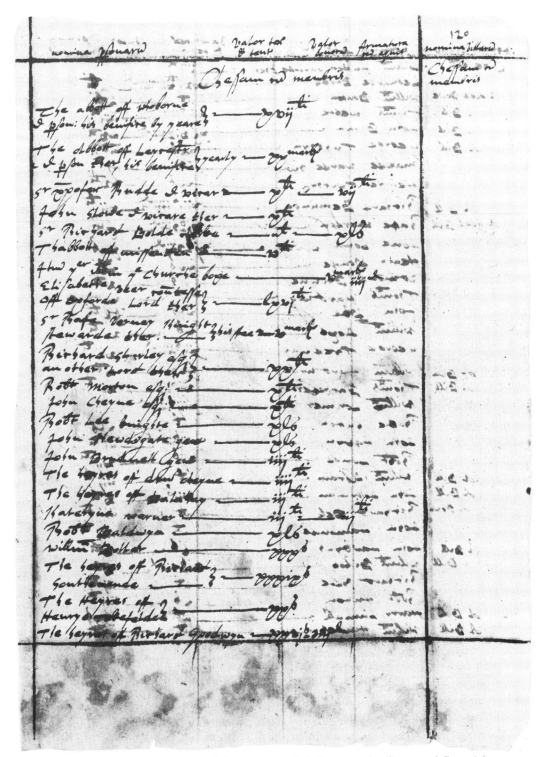

The entry for Chesham in the survey of the gentry and their tenants' military and financial resources. Ordered by Cardinal Wolsey in March 1522, it was designed to yield information to enable the raising of forced loans in the event of war with the French and Scots. (BL)

11

A muster certificate for 1595 showing the names of those serving as lancers, light horse and petronels (horsemen armed with heavy pistols) on behalf of the gentlemen listed at left, headed by Sir Robert Dormer of Wing. The liability of wealthier men to find horse was a considerable burden. (BRL)

Under The Swan 914-1792

'The mustered men for Buckingham are gone,
Under the Swan, the arms of that old town.'

Agincourt by Michael Drayton, circa 1600

Drayton's imagery in describing the assembly of Henry V's army before the expedition to Picardy in 1415 is appealing and compelling. Unfortunately, it is also highly improbable. The swan did not become associated with the county of Buckinghamshire until 1444 at the earliest, and has not been linked with any certainty before 1566. Of greater importance, mediaeval English armies were simply not raised for overseas expeditions, in the way Drayton's implies, before the mid- and late 16th century. The myth that Agincourt is the 'first battle honour' of Bucks units, based solely on the evidence of Drayton's poem, is also inscribed in the foundation plaque of the Territorial Drill Hall in Aylesbury.

Nevertheless, men from Buckinghamshire were possibly present at Agincourt, and the county probably had a military role prior to Elizabeth's reign, when Drayton actually wrote his poem. Indeed, the very creation of the county was owed to military necessities since, in 914, Edward the Elder constructed two fortresses on the Ouse at Buckingham at the beginning of his reconquest of the Danelaw, the county being the territorial basis for their maintenance. Similarly, the citizen had to undertake military service in an emergency from Anglo-Saxon times, an obligation preserved in successive mediaeval legislation such as the Assize of Arms of 1181, and the Statute of Westminster of 1285, which remained in force until the first militia statutes of 1558. Thereby counties could be required to provide levies for the English army both at home and, very occasionally, abroad. The burden fell unequally and Bucks, through its geographical position, would normally escape finding men for campaigns against the Scots or Welsh. Bucks certainly provided men for the stillborn Gascony expedition of 1295, and again for the French campaigns of 1338 and 1345, but most armies raised by the Crown for campaigns outside England were based on feudal loyalties, rather than the general obligation of the population.

The feudal system itself continued more or less to function in military terms alongside the 'national' system until the reign of Henry VIII. The great survey of the county's gentry dating from 1522 still survives; under that they were subsequently required to find tenants or others willing to serve for them in Henry's overseas expeditions. Increasingly, however, Henry looked to the country as a whole, rather than the gentry, to provide manpower, and attempted to more rigorously enforce the military training required by the Statute of Westminster. It became the practice to require musters of able-bodied men, and the increasing organisation of local forces was boosted by the coalescence of the quasi-feudal and national systems under the first militia statutes of 1558. These created a series of classes among the population according to wealth, and laid down the weapons and military equipment each was to provide. The interval between Henry's death and Elizabeth's accession also saw the beginnings of the Lieutenancy. By this, initially, groups of counties and later, single counties, were placed under the jurisdiction of a 'Lord Lieutenant'. He was charged with specific duties, such as holding regular musters and raising levies. The first person named solely for Bucks was Arthur, Lord Grey de Wilton in 1569.

The basic difference between earlier systems and that after 1558 was the Crown's increasing determination to enforce military obligations upon the citizen. Thus there was much closer scrutiny of muster certificates which purported to record the results of musters of able-bodied males. These now took place approximately every three years at convenient times such as Easter, Whitsun or Michaelmas. In theory those who defaulted were pursued; for example, Thomas Pigott of Doddershall who, in August 1587, was asked to explain why he and his servants had so far failed 'to repaire to the generall musters . . .'. Local forces were also improved by the institution of trained bands from 1573, with only a small proportion of the able-bodied selected for more concentrated training. In 1587 a total of 600 were selected in Bucks, comprising 120 pikemen, 240 calivers (early firearms), 180 bowmen and 60 billmen.

The need for this enhanced organisation was underlined by the growing threat of invasion from Spain; in 1588 Bucks contingents joined the Queen's army at Brentford, and Leicester's army at Stratford the Bow. There were further invasion scares in both 1596 and 1599, and increasing demands for levies for campaigns in the Low Countries and Ireland. Many examples can be found, such as the 47 men levied from Bucks for Ireland in September 1596. Between 1585 and 1602, Bucks contributed a total of 1,691 men to foreign expeditionary forces. Few ever returned and the county was unique in having a hospital for maimed ex-soldiers, opened at Buckingham in 1599.

The increasing demands made on counties provoked considerable local opposition and, as soon as the immediate danger had passed, in 1604 the 1558 statutes were repealed. In 1613, however, there was another Spanish invasion scare and five years later the Thirty Years War inspired yet greater urgency. The Crown's determination to modernise local forces, now generally called the militia, was associated with Royal favourite, George Villiers, Earl, Marquis and then Duke of Buckingham, and created Lord Lieutenant of Bucks in 1616. His attempt to force the gentry into greater efforts both for home defence and overseas met particular resistance. Examples included those to Flushing in 1624 and Rhé in 1627, both of which also involved greater demands for taxation in the form of 'coat and conduct money'. The men were billeted over much of southern England, which caused considerable controversy, the Provost of Eton urging Buckingham to withdraw levies from the town in 1627, since 'the youth and the soldiers do not well comport, and the town cannot easily remedy misorders'. Since the 1558 statutes had been repealed, this caused total confusion. Increasing demands were made on counties for the projected campaigns against the Scots in 1639 and 1640 and opposition grew. In Bucks there were widespread refusals to find men or money in 1640. The demand for £2,600 coat and conduct money realised only £8 10 0d. The situation was not improved by recruits destined for the army burning downing thirty houses in Aylesbury, while *en route* for Yorkshire. At Chesham the constables refused to attempt a levy, or to raise 'press' money to supply stores and victuals for the army on its march.

The militia was one of the major grievances of the House of Commons in its struggle with the Crown. The attempt to wrest control of the militia from the King, through the so-called Militia Ordinance in March 1642, contributed to the eventual civil conflict. In Bucks attempts were made both to implement the Militia Ordinance and the King's separate Commission of Array to muster the county's manpower. It was by no means easy for some individuals to make their choices in the summer of 1642; the agonised deliberations of Sir Edmund Verney of Middle Claydon and his son, Ralph, who chose opposite sides, are well known. Still others changed sides during the war, such as Sir John Borlase of Marlow, or simply preferred to leave the country, like Sir William Drake of Shardeloes. The majority of the county's gentry supported Parliament, the Bucks trained bands assembling at Aylesbury in June 1642, while the county also raised a number of regiments for the Parliamentary army, notably John Hampden's celebrated 'Greencoats'. The Bucks militia was not first raised by Henry

Bulstrode of Hedgerley in October 1642. Although Bulstrode was subsequently Parliamentary Governor of Aylesbury, his regiment raised from the Chiltern Hundreds was for service with the main army — the militia had been out since June and, of course, its origins lay far in the past.

As early as August 1642 Bucks received the first inklings of its fate over the next four years as the London Trained Bands marched through the county. A maid was accidentally shot at Wendover, 'papists' forced to provide men with meat and money in Aylesbury, Sir Alexander Denton's deer poached at Hillesden and several churches despoiled. In the same month Parliamentarians plundered Sir Richard Minshull's house at Bourton while, in November 1642, Royalists descended upon the house of Bulstrode Whitelocke, a leading parliamentarian, at Fawley Court. Gentry houses continued to suffer throughout the war, the three Royalist garrisons of Hillesden House, Greenlands House and Boarstall House all reduced by siege in March 1644, July 1644 and June 1646 respectively. The political influence of the former county élite also suffered along with houses and estates. Few of the original members of Parliament's Commission of Deputy Lieutenancy remained in the county by 1643. Some were absent with the army, such as Hampden, who was killed at Chalgrove Field in June 1643, while others like Whitelocke were occupied at Westminster. In their place, men who at most had only been lowly militia officers in 1642, such as Christopher Henn (a butcher), John Deverell (a miller), Henry Beke and Christopher Egleton (minor landowners), dominated the County Committee. Others even lower down the social scale, such as Hampden's former shepherd, Thomas Shelborne, rose to command the county's militia.

The county as a whole was caught between the Royalist stronghold at Oxford and its outposts, such as Brill, and the Parliamentary garrisons at Aylesbury and Newport Pagnell. Both sides made continual demands for money on the wretched inhabitants between. The brutality of Royalist Captain Nurse of the Hillesden garrison, who threatened the people of Stoke Hammond in December 1643 that he would not leave a piece of bread for their children's mouths, was matched by that of Parliamentarian Captain Pollard of the Newport Pagnell garrison, who 'pollarded' one unfortunate captive, while conveying him to Aylesbury. Garrisons also inflicted more immediate burdens on their unwilling hosts, the diseases spread at Newport Pagnell carrying off Cromwell's oldest son. The Governor of Newport, Sir Samuel Luke, by April 1645 feared that 'the people may rise and cut our throats', and there was something of a competition by inhabitants to get garrisons removed as fast as possible. One contemporary broadsheet remarked of Bucks that 'a man may travell into those parts and see a thousands acres and never a heard [sic] of cattel on it'.

By 1647 the country approached anarchy and there were distinct signs of social unrest. Bucks had Levellers and even Digger colonies, but was little involved in the fighting of the Second and Third Civil Wars; its economy gradually improved and its pre-war élite re-emerged. Its military forces were also reduced to one small mounted militia troop by 1656 — a kind of gendarmerie for the Major General and deputies made responsible for the county. In a real sense that was one of the supreme ironies of the Civil War and Interregnum: Parliament's triumph had, in the New Model Army, produced the very might and military depotism against which it had ostensibly fought in the first place. Inevitably, those who opposed the army increasingly saw a revival of the militia system as a natural alternative, and it was very much in this vein that the first Parliament of the restored monarchy set about re-establishing the militia in three Acts between 1661 and 1663.

As before the war, the basis of militia service remained the possession of property, with those owning estates responsible for finding men to serve on their behalf. The gentry, however, was under no statutory obligation to declare actual income, and the militia assessments were somewhat loosely interpreted. A Committee for the Militia was convened in

Bucks as early as March 1660, when it was decided to raise two troops of horse and a regiment of foot, amounting eventually to 801 foot and 158 horse. Progress thereafter was not sustained, and a body of mounted volunteers existed at Aylesbury from February 1661 until the militia was fully established. There were many tasks for the new force, such as disarming suspected rebels, and from 1663 to 1666 some part of the county's militia was always permanently on duty. The militia thus arrested suspects such as Simon Mayne of Dinton, son of the regicide, in 1683, and seized private collections of weapons in 1684 while also actively harassing dissenters. There was also a home defence role during the Dutch Wars, the Bucks militia beinng ordered out in June 1667 'at the Dutch attempt upon Chatham' and serving periods ranging from five to thirteen days at Aylesbury, Colnbrook and Newport Pagnell. The militia was, however, not very efficient: during the reign of James II it was virtually ignored while that monarch attempted to impose his will upon the country through the regular army. Regulars were thus stationed at Marlow, High Wycombe, Buckingham, Winslow, Wendover and Aylesbury as an internal police force,much as in every other county. Inevitably, the deliberate neglect of the militia, and the antagonism of the gentry towards the Crown, led to large numbers of the Bucks militia deserting to William of Orange in 1688, when he invaded, and the militia was hastily summoned by James.

The 'Glorious Revolution' did not lead to any revival of the militia's flagging fortunes. It continued to be neglected, despite the lip service paid by Parliament to its constitutional importance in relation to the standing army. Legislation lapsed and, when the militia's services were required during the Jacobite insurrections of 1715 and 1745, it proved all but impossible to summon it quickly. The last evidence of the militia in Bucks dates from 1732. In 1745, there was considerable panic in the county; Lord Cobham packed his plate at Stowe, and the streets of Chesham were barricaded with carts, waggons and beer barrels agains a foe that got no further south than Derby.

Major invasion scares always have a tendency to concentrate minds and the '45 was no exception, especially when the issue of militia reform also offered the chance of political advantage to the Opposition. It was argued that an efficient militia would be cheaper than increasing the standing army, and would also release more regulars for service overseas, obviating the need to import foreign mercenaries for home defence. A bill for militia reform was thus brought forward as early as February 1746 and again in 1752 and 1753. All failed but, with the beginning of the Seven Years War in 1755, and the usual recourse to mercenaries, agitation was revived. This eventually bore fruit in May 1757, although a further bill was required to clarify the new system in June 1758 and the militia was only made permanent by still further legislation in 1762 and 1769.

The so-called 'New Militia' envisaged a shift in the burden of military obligation, which had previously rested on property, to the lower end of the social scale. There would now be a compulsory ballot of able-bodied males aged between 18 and 50 years, with each county required to provide a quota to serve for three years. This would, in theory, ensure that each county contributed the same proportion of its manpower. In fact, the quotas were left unchanged despite population variations until 1796, that for Bucks being 560 men. There were certain exemptions from the ballot, such as articled clerks and apprentices, and those drawn might also exclude themselves by payment of a £10 fine or by finding a substitute. In some cases men joined an insurance club, in which subscriptions were used to hire substitutes for members drawn. One such operated at High Wycombe from 1762, based on a 6s policy which, by 1778, had risen to 8s. However, to pay a fine or hire a substitute was beyond the means of many, and the burden on the poor resulted in anti-militia riots. One occurred at Wing in June 1769, when a mob of over 300 prevented the ballot from taking place for the three hundreds of Cottesloe.

Despite the opposition, however, the raising of the militia proceeded, with ballots initially held at such venues as the Red Lion at High Wycombe, the Cock at Wing, the Griffin at Amersham and the Cobham Arms at Buckingham. Lists exist for seven of the county's eight hundreds from this first ballot in 1759 and reveal, not unexpectedly, that most militiamen were labourers and farm servants, who would now be compelled to appear for 20 days' continuous training (twenty eight days from 1762) each summer, during their term of service. The first Colonel of the new Bucks regiment was Sir Francis Dashwood, best remembered for his connection with the 'brotherhood' of Medmenham, the myths surrounding which owed much to his subordinate in the regiment, John Wilkes, who became a Captain. Wilkes, the MP for Aylesbury and later more notorious for the publication of the *North Briton*, succeeded Dashwood as Colonel in 1762, but was dismissed in the following year for his political activities. While he remained Colonel, however, he served with the regiment on active service; most of the new force was embodied during the latter stages of the Seven Years War for permanent wartime service. The Bucks militia was embodied at its quarters within the county in May 1760, but in March 1762 moved to Winchester for nine months before disembodiment.

At Winchester there was little to do apart from guarding French prisoners of war, although Bucks sentries prevented one large escape attempt from the King's House prison in May 1762. Most of the time was spent in 'entertainment'. The historian Edward Gibbon, who served at Winchester with the Hampshire militia, later recorded his impression of Colonel Wilkes as having:

'inexhaustible spirits, infinite wit and humour, and a great deal of knowledge; but a thorough profligate in principle as in practise; his character is infamous, his life stained with every vice, and his conversation bawdy.'

Although it stimulated the militia's establishment, the war was not a serious test of the country's defences, but the outbreak of hostilities in America in 1775 posed far more dangers, as all available regulars were dispatched there. The shock of Saratoga brought offers of new regular regiments and, in some instances, corps of volunteers were raised when France and Spain joined the war and threatened invasion in 1779. Such volunteers were not finally authorised until May 1782, the conclusion of the war in the following November ending the apparent necessity for such units. There is no evidence to suggest, as is sometimes stated, that a mounted volunteer corps was raised at Aylesbury in 1779, although it does appear that a volunteer company was raised for the militia (*ie* volunteers serving as ordinary militiamen). Moreover, the new Lord Lieutenant, George Grenville, 3rd Earl Temple, firmly rejected the plan circulated by the Earl of Shelburne in 1782 for volunteer corps. As for the militia, this had been once more embodied, spending only seventeen months in its own county between March 1778 and March 1783. The remaining months were spent at Portsmouth, Chipping Norton, Winchester, various locations in Sussex and at the great camps at Coxheath and Waterdown. Again, there were mostly prison guards to perform but, in June 1780, the regiment was brought back from Waterdown to protect the Deptford and Woolwich dockyards during the Gordon riots. Bucks detachments also guarded Lord Chesterfield's house on Blackheath against 'any outrages of the mob'.

The conclusion of the American war brought the usual demobilisation, and economies such as the extension of the term of service for militia from three to five years in 1786, and the restriction of training to only two thirds' regimental strength annually. Thus, when war once more broke out in January 1793, the immediate need was to repair the deficiencies of the past decade. This time, too, hostilities would last, with only one brief interlude, for over twenty years.

The names of Captain Tyrrel's Company of the Bucks Trained Bands, 1624/5, drawn from the three hundreds of Ashendon and Buckingham. (BRL) INSET LEFT: John Hampden. Hampden's opposition to Ship Money is well known but not his earlier defiance of the government by mustering the Bucks trained bands in the churchyard at Beaconsfield in October 1634 in contravention of the laws against the profanation of churches. (MS) RIGHT: Sir Edmund Verney, who was killed defending the Royal Standard at Edgehill in October 1642. His youngest son, Mun, was also killed in the Royal service (in 1649) while two others, Tom and Henry, spent periods as prisoners. His other son, Ralph, supported Parliament but was forced into exile from 1643 to 1650. (BB)

To the Right Honorable,

The Lords and Commons assembled in Parliament:

THE

HVMBLE PETITION

OF

The Captains, Officers, and Souldiers

of the Trained Bands, and Voluntiers of the County of
BUCKINGHAM, assembled at Alesbury, June 17. 1642.

Humbly sheweth,

THat they give you thanks from the depth of their hearts, for the great and main benefit they have already received, from Your no lesse chargeable then Indefatigable pains; And in particular, for your necessary Ordinance of the Militia, of which, as we conceive, (under God) our safety doth depend; unto which we most cheerfully submit, as is manifest by this dayes appearance; not onely of the Trained Bands, but of well neere 1000. Voluntiers, that made all demonstration of obedience, aswell to this, as to all other Commands that shall come from Your Honorable Houses, in opposition to the Popish or Malignant partie at home, or any other power from abroad; Notwithstanding the main visible discouragements from ill-affected persons, that made it their businesse, to blemish the validity of your Authority; as also, by the Lord Lieutenants absence, contrary to the Trust reposed in him.

Therefore we humbly implore the continuance of your care for our safety, and to appoint such a Lord Lieutenant in whom we may confide, as surely as you may in us, who are resolved to lay our Lives and Fortunes at your feet, in defence of the King and Parliament.

And we shall pray, &c.

---

24. JUNII.

ORdered that the Lords be moved to joyn with this House, in nominating the Lord Wharton to be Lord Lieutenant of the County of Buckingham, in stead of the Lord Paget: And that this Petition shall be forthwith printed.

H. Elsynge, Cler: Parl: D: Com:

London, Printed by L.N. and J.F. for Edward Husbands and Iohn Franck. June 25. 1642.

The petition of the Bucks Trained Bands to Parliament in June 1642 for a new Lord Lieutenant to replace Lord Paget, who had fled to join the King. (BCM)

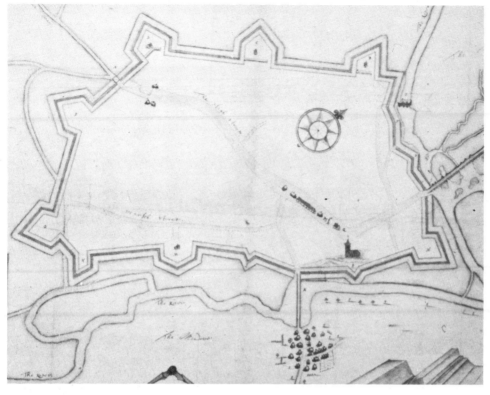

LEFT: The Parliamentary broadsheet representing the only evidence for the 'Battle of Aylesbury' on 1 November 1642. All claimed as present were conclusively elsewhere although a minor skirmish is a possibility as the Royalists advanced towards London after Edgehill. There were more substantial clashes around the town in December 1642, March 1643 and January 1644. (BCM) RIGHT: A Plan of the Defences of Newport Pagnell by Cornelius Vanden Boom, 1644. Initially garrisoned by the Royalists and then abandoned, the town was gratefully occupied by Parliamentary forces from October 1643 until the garrison was finally removed in August 1646. Some fortifications remained until 1648. (BL)

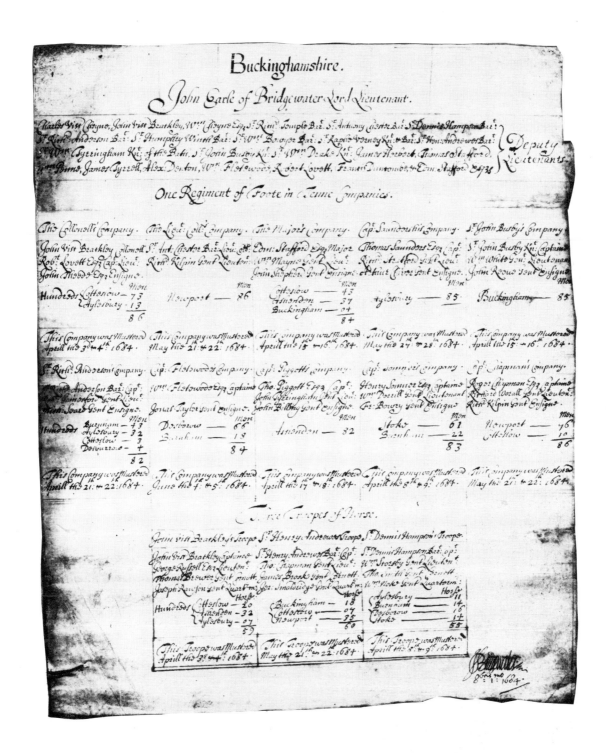

Certificate of Muster for the Bucks Militia, 1 August 1684. A total of 174 horse and 843 foot was commanded by John, Viscount Brackley. Son of the Lord Lieutenant, the 2nd Earl of Bridgewater, Brackley succeeded his father as Lord Lieutenant. He was purged in 1686 but reinstated in 1689. (PRO)

21

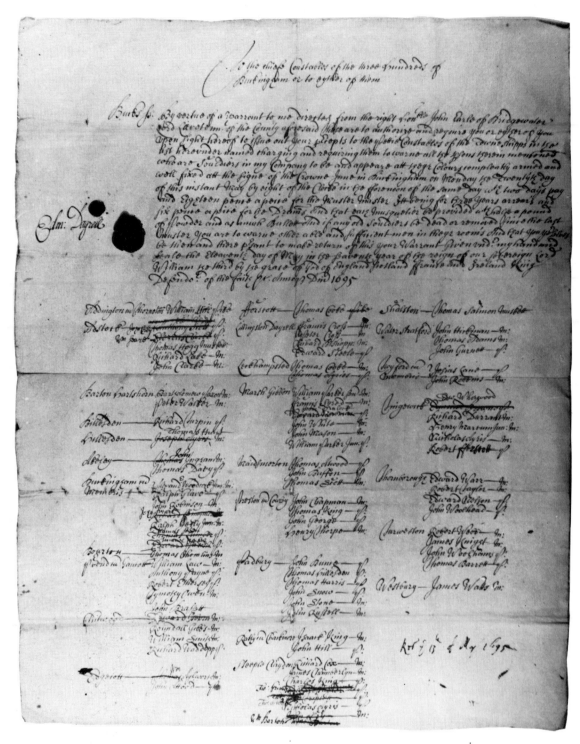

A summons issued by the Chief Constable of the three hundreds of Buckingham directing his Petty Constables to assemble Edmund Dayrell's company of militia for training at the Crown Inn, Buckingham on 20 May 1695. (CRO)

B U C K S.

Field Return of *Lt. Col. Drake's* Company of Militia this 28th Day of *April* 1760

	Captains.	Lieuts.	Ensigns.	Serjeants.	Corporals.	Drummers.	Privates.
Attending in the Field	1	1	1	2	3	2	50
On Duty	—	—	—	—	—	—	—
Absent by Leave	—	—	—	—	—	—	—
Absent without Leave	—	—	—	—	—	—	4
Sick or in Hospital	—	—	—	1	—	—	1
Dead	—	—	—	—	—	—	—
Inlisted	—	—	—	—	—	—	—
Not sworn in	—	—	—	—	—	—	—
Total Effectives	1	1	1	3	3	2	55
Wanted to compleat	—	—	—	—	—	—	—
Total Establishment	1	1	1	3	3	2	57

Wm Drake

BUCKINGHAM

LEFT: A field return for Lieutenant Colonel William Drake's company of the Bucks Militia, 28 April 1760, immediately prior to the regiment's formal embodiment at High Wycombe for war service. Drake was succeeded as Lieutenant Colonel by John Wilkes. (CRO)
RIGHT: A Bucks Militiaman, 1780. At this time the regiment ranked 45th in precedence as determined periodically by lot. In 1833 precedence was finally settled as the order in which regiments had been completed for service after 1756, Bucks ranking 35th. (NAM)

LEFT: A Battalion Officer with Colour of the Bucks Militia, 1793: a watercolour attributed to Captain Sir William Young Bt. Young, from Delaford House, almost certainly designed this new uniform, and served in the Bucks Yeomanry, for whom he wrote a drill manual and a march. (BRL) RIGHT: Richard, 4th Earl Temple (1776-1839) as Colonel Commandant of the RBKOM, 1811, from a caricature by Denis Dighton: he commanded 1803-1839. In France with the 1st Provisional Battalion in 1814 he and fellow officers were nicknamed 'les boeufs-gros anglais' after their sheer bulk. BELOW: Young's watercolour of the artillery attached to the Bucks Militia, 1793. Two six pounders were attached but, in 1794, surplus funds from county subscriptions were used to purchase two twelve pounders and to add forty artillerymen. The two 'county' guns are now at Fort Ticonderoga Museum, New York State. (BRL)

24

The Grenville Factor 1793-1815

The chief inspiration behind the defence of Bucks during the French Revolutionary and Napoleonic Wars was one man — George Grenville, 3rd Earl Temple and 1st Marquis of Buckingham (1753-1813). Frustrated in national politics through his own unstable temperament, Buckingham remained avaricious for both recognition and influence. He thus determinedly pursued the garter (achieved in 1786) and a dukedom (achieved only by his son) in the cause of the former and dominated his county in the cause of the latter. His first connection with the county's military affairs was in 1778, when he obtained a militia commission and became Lieutenant Colonel in 1780. The county Lieutenancy in 1782 was an even greater prize, and it was in that capacity that one clergyman wrote of Buckingham in 1797 that 'no County can boast of a more active Lord Lieutenant'. To be fair to him, the county did occupy an important strategic position astride the main routes to London, as he was to remind the government more than once.

With the approach of war, the militia was embodied in December 1792. Since most regulars would be required overseas, the force represented the main defence against the raids envisaged and actually planned by the French Convention. As in previous wars, however, the militia was not available for local defence and, between 1793 and 1798 alone, the Bucks Militia passed through Winchester, Weymouth, Southsea, Portsea, Bristol and Chelmsford. There it performed the usual mundane garrison duties, though its tour at Weymouth in 1794 (where the King had repaired for the bathing), earned the title 'Royal Bucks King's Own' Militia from 26 September 1794. Service in large towns also brought contact with radical elements. At Portsmouth in July 1796, the flogging of a private for drunkenness and striking an officer brought demonstrations of sympathy from dockyard workers, who displayed effigies of the 'murthering Marquis'. Patience and discipline were greatly taxed, but at Bristol in May 1797 a seditious handbill brought reassuring declarations of loyalty from NCOs, who denied alleged grievances which 'some designing Villains' had circulated. Unlike others, the Royal Bucks did not suffer great indiscipline.

Disaffection was understandable; a strong link persisted between society and militiaman until discipline brought a force of almost exclusively manual workers under control. In February 1797, for example, 113 men served in the Royal Bucks for the three hundreds of Newport; some 68 of the 97 whose occupations are known were labourers. This reliance on manual workers did not materially change. Incomplete courts martial books record 171 separate offences committed between 1793 and 1795, including 61 cases of unauthorised absence from parades or quarters, 30 cases of theft, 28 of drunkenness, one of accusing a fellow soldier of an 'unnatural crime', and an instance of maliciously wounding a cow. Joseph Mayett, a Quainton labourer who served in the Royal Bucks from 1803 to 1815 and left a fascinating autobiography, records how a small group of practising Nonconformists was subjected to some harrassment by their comrades and nicknamed the 'soapy set'. Despite his religious beliefs, Mayett himself frequently succumbed to temptation, as well as to periodic bouts of illness, including small pox and 'white flux', as the regiment progressed from one garrison to another.

Nevertheless, the militia generally proved entirely trustworthy in later social, economic and political disturbances, although there were always lingering doubts about allowing it to serve in its own areas. Thus the machine-breaking disturbances in the north of England in 1812 led to the employment of southern militia; the Royal Bucks was stationed at Woodbridge, Nottingham, Manchester and Newcastle-upon-Tyne from January 1812 to April 1813. However, this was not the limit of its services, since the Marquis was keen to see service abroad. He had offered to take the regiment to the Channel Islands in 1793 and, resisting suggestions that militiamen should be recruited to the army in 1798, proposed they serve in Ireland, where rebellion had broken out. Legislation was passed and the regiment became the first to arrive in Ireland in July 1798. It was a trying period for both Buckingham, angered at being left in Dublin when a French expeditionary force landed to assist the rebels, and for his men, who suffered disease, attempted subversion and murder. The Royal Bucks returned to England in May 1799, but Buckingham again offered to lead it to the Texel in September. His son, Richard, 4th Earl Temple, who succeeded to his command in 1803, when Buckingham withdrew through ill health, also offered to take the regiment abroad, in 1808 and 1810. He did take it to Ireland again in May 1813 and, while most of the regiment remained there until October 1814, Temple took 470 men to Bordeaux in March 1814 as part of the 1st Provisional Battalion attached to Wellington's army; they were too late to fight.

Despite the opposition of commanding officers like Buckingham and Temple, the militia was raided for regular recruits in 1799, 1804-1805, 1807, 1809 and from 1811 to 1814. This and other wastage, such as desertion, meant that counties had to find a fairly continuous flow of recruits to fill the gaps. Buckingham's brother, Lord Grenville, reported in June 1803 that Bucks parishes were complaining 'grieviously of the desertions in the Militia', while Buckingham himself complained in 1807 of the detrimental impact of insurance societies in the south of Bucks. Parishes also complained of the cost of upkeep of militiamen's families on the rates. Some £2,000 had been expended on militia families between 1758 and 1764, and it had been described as the greatest burden on farmers between 1778 and 1782. By 1800 it was costing the county over £3,500 per annum.

Further grievances resulted from the many temporary expedients introduced by successive governments to meet manpower deficiencies. In 1796, following Spain's entry into the war against Britain, a Provisional Cavalry reverted to the pre-1757 concept of obligation upon property; one man and one horse were levied for every ten horses kept for riding or carriage drawing. The Bucks quota was 186 men, while a further 662 men comprised the county quota for a Supplementary Militia that same year. Over the country as a whole, 60,000 men were to be raised for the latter by ballot, and trained for 20 day periods in contingents of one twentieth of total strength. Another idea was for some kind of *levée en masse* of the able-bodied male population. This originated in Dorset in 1797, where the High Sheriff listed all capable of undertaking service in an emergency in the ancient *posse comitatus* (civil power of the county). As a result of publicity, this was emulated in Northumberland and, through Buckingham's interest, in Bucks between February and March 1798. It also attracted government support with the Defence of the Realm Act in April 1798, requiring the listing of inhabitants, livestock, and vehicles.

The same concept was revived in the first Defence Act of June 1803, which required the listing of those aged 15 to 60, and the second General Defence Act of July 1803, which required returns of those aged 17 to 55, divided into classes according to age and marital status. Three years later, the Training Act proposed calling up all able-bodied English males between 16 and 40, and training them in batches of 200,000, on 26 days per annum. Two other measures attempted to draft men into the army for home service. The Army of Reserve (also known as the Additional Army of England) of 1803 sought to find 50,000 men for five years' service through ballot. The Permanent Additional Force Act, in operation from June 1804 to May 1806 and effectively absorbing both Army of Reserve and Supplementary Militia, eschewed a ballot, but compelled parishes to provide recruits. They received a bounty of one guinea for every man recruited, but were liable to a £20 fine for every man short.

In Bucks, as elsewhere, those measures enforced by ballot were highly unpopular, Wing again witnessing an anti-militia riot in December 1796, as a wave of unrest similar to that of 1757 greeted the ballot for the Supplementary Militia. The Army of Reserve, for which the county quota was 435 men, was particularly resented, with insurance clubs swiftly emerging at Stoke Poges, Eton and Upton in August 1803. Attempts to avoid the ballot also pushed up the price of Bucks substitutes to as much as £40 by December 1803. In one case, Butler Stevens, a Bledlow labourer, was brought to court by John Gough, a Princes Risborough grocer. He had offered Stevens 22 guineas, and given him 5s 0d in advance plus 3s 0d worth of ribbons, and all he could drink at the inn where he hired him, as a substitute for the Army of Reserve. Subsequently, Stevens had refused to serve. Another means of evading the militia was voluntary service, and this was eagerly seized upon.

Exemption was first granted to infantry volunteers and their mounted yeomanry equivalents in 1794 but, by contrast, those associations formed in 1797 were not given exemption. Nor were those enlisted after October 1796 exempt from the Supplementary Militia ballot (until 1799) but, in April 1798, all volunteers and yeomanry were exempted from the milita ballot, provided they were prepared to serve throughout a military district. In addition, yeomanry was exempted from horse duty from 1795, and both yeomanry and volunteers were exempted from hair powder duty from 1800. Those opting to continue their services after the Peace of Amiens retained their exemptions and, with the renewal of war in May 1803, exemption remained an attractive card for the government to play. In 1797 the Bucks yeomanry was doubled through the belief that the Provisional Cavalry would be dropped if sufficient volunteers came forward. Similarly, operation of the Defence Act of July 1803 was suspended where volunteers equal to three quarters of those listed in the first class came forward. Yeomanry and volunteers serving prior to June 1803 were exempt from the Army of Reserve and, when infantry volunteers were largely replaced by a Local Militia in 1808, a ballot for this force was again suspended where six times the militia quota (of 1802) volunteered. Even the militia ballot itself was suspended from 1806 to 1807, and again from 1811 to 1813.

To some extent, then, volunteering was self-interest. It has also been argued that volunteers and yeomanry came about as much in response to the threat of domestic insurrection as to that of invasion. In the case of Bucks, units raised between 1794 and 1803 consciously fulfilled both purposes. Legislation in March 1794 allowed for the augmentation of the militia, and for accepting volunteer offers. A public meeting held at Aylesbury on 3 May 1794 resolved to open a subscription to raise troops of 'Armed Yeomanry'. In common with other counties, only surplus funds would be devoted to militia augmentation, the cost of which was chiefly borne by Buckingham and the Earl of Chesterfield. By the summer, yeomanry troops had been established at Amersham, Aylesbury, Buckingham, Burnham, High Wycombe and Newport Pagnell. In accordance with the avowed intention to 'preserve domestic tranquility', detachments attended markets at Aylesbury and Newport Pagnell in April 1795, to prevent grain riots; dispersed mobs trying to stop grain waggons at Stony Stratford and Fenny Stratford in March 1796; suppressed the anti-militia disturbance at Wing and, in a further wave of food riots in 1800, stood by in case of trouble at Leckhampstead in May and at Burnham in October.

The Bucks infantry volunteers also regarded themselves primarily as a constabulary force. In February 1797 Buckingham received authority to add small infantry corps to the yeomanry, comprising 'respectable inhabitants . . . whose situation and occupations do not allow them to serve on horseback'. Amounting to 127 men at Aylesbury, Buckingham, Eton, Olney and Newport Pagnell by June, these units were to 'give effectual protection to property'. Under the Defence of the Realm Act, some 625 men had been enrolled as volunteers at Newport Pagnell by 1 May 1798, a further 158 at Aylesbury and Buckingham by 14 May, and 937 men in eight companies by September, while the yeomanry had attained a strength of 770 men in sixteen troops. In some counties, volunteers proved unreliable in the food disturbances of 1800-1801. This was not the case in Bucks, although evidence suggests that, as elsewhere, volunteers were drawn from a lower social class than originally intended. Labourers certainly offered themselves as volunteers at Dinton and Stone in 1803, and the general reluctance of men to come forward in south Bucks in August 1803 drew the comment from Buckingham that 'the lower classes are stated to me to be utterly disinclined to voluntary offers', indicating that he expected them to be volunteers.

The yeomanry, of course, defined themselves as the farming community although, in Bucks, the yeomanry was not exclusively dependent on them. Although there were 54 farmers among 78 yeomen at Aylesbury in 1800, only 19 of 96 men in the Burnham and Stoke Squadron were farmers in June 1798, the remainder being gentlemen, professional men and tradesmen. There was, however, a dependence upon the unchanging pattern of the agricultural year, hence the frequent allusion to the farming season in contemporary military correspondence. In September 1797, for example, exercises were postponed due to a late harvest, while in the 1st or Southern Regiment of Bucks Yeomanry, the annual inspection was held in July rather than August 1812 due to the 'state of the harvest'; other exercises in 1813 and 1814 were arranged to avoid clashing with Epsom races and Wycombe market. After 1808, the Local Militia held its annual training in May, to suit farmers 'whose servants were mostly in' the force.

Both yeomanry and volunteers largely governed themselves with discipline through fines. The original officers of the Bucks yeomanry in 1794 were all elected, and subsequently drew lots for seniority when the appointments were belatedly gazetted in 1795. Such arrangements, and the concession to local circumstances, were due to the lack of any officially defined terms of service. Indeed, the Iver Volunteers were so bewildered by the terms offered by the government in 1803 that they refused to take the oath of loyalty, and were disbanded in September. Those volunteers raised in 1794 were entitled to pay for two days' training a week, but those raised in 1797 received no pay, and those raised in 1798 received one day's pay per week. With the Peace of Amiens those units continuing to serve received no pay, while units raised after the renewal of hostilities in 1803 could be governed either by the 'June allowances', with pay for up to 85 days a year, or the 'August allowances', offering only 20 days' pay. Consolidating legislation in 1804 restricted all to 24 days' pay per annum but failed to remove differences in liability between June and August volunteers. Most units depended upon public subscription to supplement such grants. This was not always successful, and in Bucks the yeomanry had debts of over £3,000 by 1798, since many of the sums promised in 1794 did not materialise. By compensation, Buckingham and his family were generous.

Of course, the Grenvilles also dominated the appointments in the auxiliary forces, which represented a considerable source of patronage, at least in terms of prestige. After September 1803, when the volunteers and yeomanry were both reorganised into three regiments — a 1st or Southern, 2nd or Mid and 3rd or Northern Bucks regiment in each case — Lord Grenville commanded the 1st Southern Regiment of yeomanry from 1803 to 1807 and his brother, Thomas Grenville, commanded the 2nd Mid Bucks yeomanry from 1803 to 1813.

Buckingham was, of course, commandant of militia, yeomanry and volunteers while his son, Temple, was a major in the yeomanry as well as commander of the militia from 1803 onwards. In 1803 the three yeomanry regiments totalled 1,126 men and the volunteers 2,426 men.

Despite the degree of self-sufficiency, the auxiliaries still cost government large sums of money which, coupled with the conflicting allowances, was sufficient to require further consolidation. A determined assault was mounted on the volunteers, though not the yeomanry, by William Windham as Secretary at War from 1806-7. He removed clothing allowances and reduced the number of training days for which pay could be claimed. Unfortunately, Windham also removed the inducement to efficiency by eliminating the threat of the ballot. His successor, Lord Castlereagh, initially solved the problem by the creation of the Local Militia in 1808. Enlisted for four years (renewed in 1812), with a continuous 28 day period of annual training, the Local Militia would be filled by ballot of those aged 18-30 years without substitution or insurance, and with heavy fines for exemption. Volunteers were encouraged to transfer for a two guinea bounty, and Buckingham urged all to do so in order to spare the county from a ballot; the total number required was set at 3,594 men, or six times the militia quota of 1802. All the northern regiment and two-thirds of the others transferred, but this still amounted to only 894 men and, after the permitted addition of the 1,281 yeomen, a further 1,429 men had to be found by voluntary means or ballot. Elsewhere those remaining volunteer units lost further allowances in 1809, and were ordered to be disbanded in March 1813, so that their weapons could be supplied to Prussia.

The dispatch of British arms to Prussia itself indicated that home defence was no longer essential, following the defeat of French armies and aspirations. As a result, the auxiliary forces also wound down, and the thanks of Parliament for wartime services were conveyed to the county's forces by Temple, now 2nd Marquis of Buckingham and Lord Lieutenant, in July 1814.

Mansel Dawkin Mansel as Captain and Adjutant of the Bucks Yeomanry, 1799. Mansel of Lavendon House acted as adjutant for the yeomanry as a whole from 1797 to 1802 and thereafter for the northern regiment as well as acting as adjutant for the northern volunteer infantry. A banker, he committed suicide when his Newport Pagnell bank failed in 1822. (AMOT)

The ARTICLES of ENROLMENT,

Armed Yeomanry of the County of Bucks,

For the Internal Defence and Security of the *Kingdom*,
during the present *War*.

I. To receive no Pay, unlefs when embodied or callep out; but to attend mounted on a serviceable Gelding or Mare, to be approved of by the Commanding Officer of each Troop, and not lefs than fourteen hands high, for the purpose of Meeting at such Times and Places as shall be fixed by such Commanding Officer, with the Approbation of the Field Officer commanding the whole body.

II. The times and places of Meeting to be fixed on such days, and at such hours of the day as may interfere the leaft with the other Avocations of the Persons composing the refpective Troops.

III. The Corps to be fubject to be embodied within the County, by special direction from His Majesty, on Appearance of Invasion; and to be called out of the County by the like authority from His Majesty in case of Actual Invasion.

IV. To be liable to be called upon by Order from His Majesty, or by the Lord Lieutenant, or by the Sheriff of the County, for the fuppreffion of Riots and Tumults within the County.

V. In all Cases when embodied or called out as above, to receive Pay as Cavalry, and to be fubject to the provisions of the Mutiny Bill.

1794

Bucks Committee.

At a Meeting held in PARLIAMENT STREET, this 27th of *May*, 1794,—the following Resolution was ordered to be printed and circulated:

RESOLVED,

" THAT this Committee having held several Meetings for the purpose of considering the several points referred to them, and having digested certain Rules for the formation of the Corps of the

Armed Yeomanry of the County of Bucks,

and having directed certain Articles to be provided for their Equip-

OPPOSITE ABOVE: The Articles of Enrolment for the Bucks Yeomanry as adopted 3 May 1794. Particularly significant were articles 2 and 3, stressing attention to the convenience of members and concern with domestic unrest. (CRO) BELOW: Resolutions of the County Committee, consisting of all who subscribed over £20 to the general fund as well as delegates from towns, for the recruitment of the Yeomanry. Advertisements were also placed in newspapers by the Committee sitting at No. 6, Parliament Street, the London offices of the Grand Junction Canal Company. (CRO) ABOVE LEFT: John Penn as Captain in the Eton Troop, 1st or Southern Regiment of Bucks Yeomanry Cavalry, 1809; he suffered from St Vitus' dance, lived at Stoke Park and was the High Sheriff charged with the compilation of the *posse comitatus* in 1798. (AMOT) RIGHT: Sir Thomas Tyringham Bernard (1792-1883) in the uniform of the Bucks Local Militia, 1816; of Nether Winchendon House, he entered the Local Militia on coming down from Oxford, later joined the 2nd or Mid Bucks Yeomanry in 1819, and was Lieutenant Colonel of the latter from 1843 to 1862. (SB)

We, the underwritten, who had formed ourselves into an Association, for learning the use of Arms, in order to cooperate with our fellow Countrymen, in the protection of all that is dear to us, against all Invaders whatever, consider with due regret the obstructions that is thrown in the way of our progress, by our having no person among us able, & willing to take the Command; But still approving our design, and wishing to give them Effect, engage to hold ourselves in Readiness to come forward, should the difficulties under which we labor be removed, in which respect we have heretofore set our Hands, this 10th of Septr. 1798. —

Resolutions of a meeting to form a military association at Chesham, 20 June 1798 failed when the prospective commander, a tanner named George Hepburn, withdrew in September and no other candidates presented themselves. (BB)

To the Inhabitants of the Town
AND
Neighbourhood of Aylesbury.

THE Committee appointed by the late Meeting of the Inhabitants, for carrying into Effect their Resolution, for raising a MILITARY ASSOCIATION, amongst themselves; think it their first Duty to publish for general Consideration the following Outlines of the Plan, upon which they have judged it advisable that such a Corps should be raised.

FIRST.—They, without Hesitation, entirely disclaim all paltry Party Motives; considering, that whilst the WOLVES OF FRANCE are howling at the Doors of the English Family, the petty Quarrels of the Children should cease. The Safety of our good old KING, the Chastity of our Wives, our Sisters, and our Daughters, The Property we possess, whether in a Palace, a House, a Cottage, or a Chest, *We will Fight to Preserve*: We will not suffer the Officers of an Army of Frenchmen to become our Gentry, in Lieu of those who were bred amongst ourselves; nor will we suffer the common Soldiers of Savage France, their Wives and Children by conquering us, and settling themselves here to become our Manufacturers, the Labourers in our Fields, and the Gatherers of our Harvest, instead of the honest, sturdy, generous English Poor, who shall not be driven out or starved, to flatter French Vanity and Impudence.

SECONDLY.—The Committee declare, That as the Virtues, Talents, & Valour of the Man who enters into this Corps, are what they will respect and admire, more than his Gentility

Bucks Local Militia.

Three Hundreds of Cottesloe.

I *William Welch* do make Oath that I am by my Trade a *Carpenter* and have been usually resident in the Parish of *Whitchurch* in the County of *Bucks* — that I am — married and that I have no Children and that I have no Rupture, nor ever was troubled with Fits; and am no ways disabled by Lameness or otherwise; but have the perfect use of my Limbs; and that I am not a Seaman or Seafaringman, As witness my Hand at *Aylesbury* the *26th* Day of *October* one thousand eight hundred and *twelve*

The Mark ✕ of *William Welch*

Sworn before me at *Aylesbury* this *26th* Day of *October* one thousand eight hundred and *twelve*

Witness present,

ABOVE: Resolutions for raising the Loyal Aylesbury Volunteers, 1803 in response to the government's Defence Act. The desire to avoid the ballot under the legislation is noticeably unstated, although the age range of 17-55 years betrays it. (CRO) LEFT: A drum of the Amersham Armed Association said to have been carried by Sergeant Major Berry, landlord of the Griffin, 1806. RIGHT: One of the declarations required of all volunteers and ballotted men enrolled in the 2nd or Mid Bucks Regiment of Local Militia for the Cottesloe Sub-division, October to December 1812. (CRO)

LEFT: Sir William Clayton Bt as Lt Colonel Commandant of the 1st or Southern Regiment of Bucks Yeomanry Cavalry, 1820-1828. Clayton of Harleyford Manor was originally elected to command of the Marlow Troop in 1797, succeeding Lord Grenville in command of the 1st Regiment in 1807 and serving on until its demise, at which he was aged 68 years. (BB) RIGHT: Richard, 2nd Duke of Buckingham and Chandos (1797-1861) as Colonel Commandant of the 2nd Regiment of Bucks Yeomanry Cavalry, 1841. Better known by his earlier title of Marquis of Chandos, he lavished his fortune on the regiment and especially its uniforms. Chandos introduced the hussar uniform in 1821. (NAM)

Laws and Disorders 1815-1850

The end of the conflicts between 1793 and 1815 inevitably left a legacy of anti-militarism and a desire for military retrenchment. Yet not all vestiges of the auxiliary forces were removed. Some disappeared, but others survived, even if in a moribund state, until the perception of national danger led to a revival in the 1840s.

The Local Militia ballot was suspended in May 1816, thus effectively ending the force's existence, the suspension renewed annually until 1836, when legislation lapsed. Yet, in the curious manner in which elements of the amateur military tradition lingered on, the Local Militia Act of 1812 remained on the statute book until 1921, while the Training Act of 1806 survived until 1875. The 1804 Yeomanry and Volunteer Consolidation Act continued to govern any volunteers until 1863, while the yeomanry, which largely survived post-war reductions, was still governed under its provisions until 1901. Moreover, even the militia survived as an institution, for all that it appeared not to be functioning at all after the 1830s.

The militia was, of course, disembodied, the Royal Bucks returning from its last station at Fort Cumberland, Portsmouth in January 1816. However, the permanent staffs of adjutants and NCOs remained in being throughout the next forty years, even if reduced in establishment, as in 1829 and 1835, or when all arms were returned to store in February 1836. The political issue of the merits of compulsion over voluntary enlistment in the militia also remained very much alive. A ballot was held in 1816, although no training took place until 1820 and 1821, lists of those enrolled in Bucks in 1821 demonstrating the continued dependence upon labourers. Training was also ordered in 1825, when the term of service was extended to five years, and a ballot was held in 1828, only to be suspended in the following year. Prevailing political unrest saw yet another ballot revival in 1830, with training ordered for 1831, but opposition, especially from the National Union of the Working Classes, was considerable. The Union argued that those without the franchise could not be expected to undertake compulsory service for those who did possess a vote. There was also a moral challenge to militarism from nonconformist groups, and the NUWC's theme was echoed by a variety of working class organisations in the 1840s. As a result, successive governments fought shy of compulsion, which was not re-introduced in any form until 1916.

Although no training was held after 1831, the militia still functioned as a social institution, at least in terms of its officer corps. New appointments continued to be made — fifteen in Bucks between 1815 and 1852 — and the militia's status remained of account in county society. Thus the 1st Duke of Buckingham and Chandos unsuccessfully attempted to remove three officers in January 1831 whose mercantile connections he judged unsuitable. Similarly, Robert, 2nd Lord Carrington (1796-1868), who succeeded the Duke as Lord Lieutenant in 1839, clearly regarded the militia as a great prize, since he reputedly paid an ailing Duke some £2,000 for the colonelcy in 1839, when the militia's future was dim. Assuming command on 7 March 1839, Carrington took only four days to transfer the staff and headquarters to his own seat at Wycombe Abbey, from the fine barracks built in Buckingham in 1802. The symbolism was not lost on the Grenvilles, the 3rd Duke immediately enquiring into the legality of the transfer when he, in turn, succeeded Carrington as Lord Lieutenant in 1868.

The Grenvilles had themselves demonstrated the uses to which the militia staff might be put while they still controlled the regiment. Thus, in 1830, the fourteen members of the Corporation of Buckingham (the entire electorate) included the quartermaster, paymaster, adjutant and former adjutant of the Royal Bucks, the adjutant acting in addition as town clerk. Carrington, who was also resented as a newcomer whose family thirty years previously 'was a stranger to the county without an acre in it', unashamedly filled the officer corps with his relatives. He did, however, maintain its élitist nature, the militia as a whole probably surviving unreformed for so long because of its social significance to an aristocracy fearful of losing its influence elsewhere. Other factors of importance were the political strength of the militia's representatives in Parliament, and the failure of politicians to agree on what form militia service should take, so that a variety of proposals failed to gain sufficient political support between 1827 and 1852.

Despite the loss of the militia, the Grenvilles still had adequate prestige through the yeomanry, which was far more visible to society than a militia largely represented at county functions by a small permanent staff. All three Bucks yeomanry regiments remained in being in 1815, amounting to 683 men in 22 troops by 1817. The force still fulfilled a number of purposes, not least in providing sheer spectacle. This had been equally true of the Napoleonic period, Edmund Waller of Hall Barn complaining in 1809 that the crowds who had come to watch yeomanry exercises had extensively damaged his property. After the war, the summer 'trials of skill' and 'trials of speed' held by the 2nd Mid Bucks Regiment at Stowe in the 1820s became a highly popular entertainment. Larger reviews included a visit to Stowe by the Duke of Wellington in December 1827, one by Queen Adelaide in August 1840 and, most significant of all, that by Queen Victoria to Stowe in January 1845. Then there were the annual training periods, usually for eight days and usually in May, with troops often split between a number of venues such as Newport Pagnell, Olney and Fenny Stratford for the 3rd or Northern Regiment and Aylesbury, Buckingham and Winslow for the 2nd Regiment. The trade generated was sufficient for High Wycombe and Beaconsfield to actually compete for the visit of the 1st or Southern Regiment in 1825.

But the yeomanry fulfilled more than a decorative purpose in the years of social, economic and political unrest that followed Waterloo. Primarily such unrest was in northern or midland urban areas and, with the exception of East Anglia, rural disturbances were comparatively rare. Nevertheless, the 2nd or Mid Bucks Regiment was put on alert for possible use in 1817 and 1819 and, two years later, both the 1st and 2nd Regiments were employed on guard duties in London during the coronation of George IV in July 1821, due to the King's unpopularity in the Queen Caroline affair. However, there was a widespread belief, even in conservative circles, that the yeomanry was not ideal for aid to the civil power. It was not trained in such duty, was widely believed to be less than impartial and its presence often exacerbated rather than defused disturbances. Since the yeomanry also received army pay for aid to the civil power, from 1817 onwards, it was also costly to employ while riots tended to occur at just those moments in the agricultural year when farmers found it inconvenient to be absent for long.

There are occasional echoes of this criticism of the yeomanry in Bucks, and of the problems faced in calling out the force. In 1821, for example, the 2nd Marquis of Buckingham rewarded those of his tenants who had 'suffered much inconvenience, by absenting themselves from their farms at so busy a time' for coronation duty, by suspending payment of rents due at Michaelmas until the following Lady Day. He was also distressed to record that the only overt hostility displayed towards the yeomanry during this duty had been at Aylesbury and, not as might be expected, in London. The Bucks press contained, too, periodic attacks on the yeomanry as a weapon of reaction, as in 1827 and 1831. Given such criticism and the search for economy, it is perhaps not surprising that the force found itself the victim of retrenchment in December 1827, when it was announced that all those regiments that had not been called out in aid of the civil power in the previous ten years would be disbanded. The coronation duty not being counted, all three Bucks regiments qualified for disbandment, and in April 1828 the 1st and 3rd Regiments ceased to exist, at which time they consisted of 229 men in eight troops and 321 men in four troops respectively. Through the determination and financial support of the Marquis of Chandos, later 2nd Duke of Buckingham and Chandos, the 2nd Mid Bucks was allowed to serve on without pay or allowances, although retaining exemption from the ballot. Now officially known as the 2nd Regiment of Bucks Yeomanry Cavalry, it was reorganised with six of the original troops and two new ones raised at Olney and Newport Pagnell to cover the recruiting ground of the former 3rd Regiment. By 1832 a troop had also been raised at Chesham and High Wycombe in the old 1st Regiment area.

The cost of maintaining the regiment contributed in no small way to the 2nd Duke's eventual bankruptcy in 1848, but its continuance proved highly fortuitous when, just three years later, many of the counties that had lost their yeomanry in 1827 were subjected to the widespread agricultural disturbances known as the 'Swing riots'. 'Swing' was occasioned by population growth in rural areas placing additional pressure on an overcrowded labour market, already vulnerable to the introduction of labour saving devices such as threshing machines. This stimulated greater unemployment and greater poverty at a time of poor harvest and rising prices, while there was also a concerted attempt by the wealthy to reduce their expenditure on the poor rates. Other local factors could be involved, such as the equal concern among journeymen paper manufacturers in Bucks at the introduction of machinery in the paper mills around High Wycombe. The main disturbances spread into Bucks on 11 November 1830, when threatening letters were received by gentry and farmers at Colnbrook, Langley and High Wycombe. In all, there were 39 separate incidents between 11 November and 9 December, involving 18 cases of machines of one kind or another being destroyed.

The 2nd Bucks had, in fact, already been out that autumn, assisting the Oxfordshire Yeomanry in enclosure disturbances on Otmoor on 6 September 1830, and the 276 men of the regiment were then almost continuously on duty from 22 November until 7 December. Detachments visited Aylesbury, Brill, Buckingham, High Wycombe, Hounslow, Marlow, Princes Risborough and Whitchurch. In addition, yeomen were included in the 50 men guarding the Marquis of Chandos' house at Wotton Underwood, and a detachment helped defend the 1st Duke's house at Avington in Hampshire on 22 November, special dispensation being granted them to go there by that county's Lord Lieutenant, the Duke of Wellington. It did not prove easy for farmers to be out for long, only four men answering one summons to Whitchurch. Chandos was to claim that it was only in Aylesbury that his men 'had not been even flatteringly received', the regiment's quarters at the George being stoned during a brief halt there on 22 November, but a squadron was also sent away by High Wycombe magistrates for fear of further inflaming the mob on 26 November. In the event, order at Wycombe was restored by Special Constables, members of the King's Staghounds who happened to be in the neighbourhood, and six Guardsmen sent from Windsor in post chaises. Special Constables, authorised under 1817 legislation, were also raised in a number of other towns, including Newport Pagnell and Marlow, while the Duke encouraged associations for the protection of property. An 'Association of Volunteer Mounted Constables' was enrolled at High Wycombe in December, and night patrols and farm guards were also reported at Chesham and Upton.

In January 1831 the King's Commission sat at Aylesbury to try 137 of those apprehended. The yeomanry was again called out from 9 to 15 January with detachments stationed at Aston Clinton, Bierton, Brill, Long Crendon, Quainton, Stone, Weedon, Wendover, Whitchurch, and especially at Waddesdon. In addition, the 16 members of the militia permanent staff were placed inside Aylesbury Gaol with two artillery pieces, with 20 Pensioners next door in the House of Correction, and 200 Special Constables in the town. The Sheriff, Richard Howard-Vyse, hazarded that this was probably 'sufficient', and the Duke was only reluctantly persuaded by a government adviser to allow half the yeomanry home: others were also allowed leave for Buckingham fair. There was no trouble.

As a result of the Swing riots, the 2nd Regiment of Bucks Yeomanry Cavalry was returned to full pay from 17 December 1830, but its temporary absence from the official list of corps gave the regiment only 21st place in precedence. (This was established in 1885 on the basis of official continuous service.) A new independent troop was also authorised on 27 December 1830. Briefly known as the Marlow Troop, it soon became retitled the Taplow Troop or South Bucks Yeomanry Cavalry. Its first service was at Princes Risborough during the sitting of the King's Commission. Further calls on the Bucks yeomen were to be made in both 1835 and 1848. Two troops were required in May 1835 to ensure the successful transfer of paupers from Chesham to the new poor house at Amersham, in accordance with the consolidation required by the New Poor Law. The change in the customary administration of poor relief had resulted in the same angry reaction that had characterised the equally retrospective protest involved in Swing. In April 1848 it relieved regular troops from Hounslow and Windsor, for duty during the Chartist demonstration planned for London. The majority of the regiment relieved the 12th Lancers at Hounslow, but the Newport Pagnell and Olney Squadron had the unique duty of taking over from the Household Cavalry at Windsor Castle.

Between the two spells of duty in aid of the civil power, distrust of the yeomanry and the search for further economy saw the Taplow Troop struck off the official establishment in May 1838. Like the 2nd Regiment in 1827, the Taplow Troop served on without pay or allowances, until a deteriorating political climate allowed it to return to the establishment of yeomanry in April 1843. The troop offered its services in anticipation of Chartist demonstrations at Slough in 1848 but was not required, the agitation met by Special Constables. No Bucks auxiliary unit was to undertake duties in aid of the civil power again, successive governments looking increasingly to other alternatives. Pensioners were toyed with as a quasi-police force in the 1840s, but it was the steady establishment of the police force itself that did most to remove the contentious issue of amateur soldiers in conflict with their fellow citizens. County police forces were authorised under the Rural Constabulary Act of 1839, but it was not until 1857 that Bucks formed its county police. This was in compliance with the compulsory requirements of the County and Borough Police Act of 1856, which owed much to fears of potential havoc wrought by soldiers returning from the Crimea.

It was, of course, also a measure of the changing nature of British society that troops were required less in aid of the civil power by the end of the 1840s. But if the auxiliary forces had lost one, albeit unwanted, function, the traditional role of home defence was to become a reality once more, as national perceptions led to demands for the revival of both militia and volunteers.

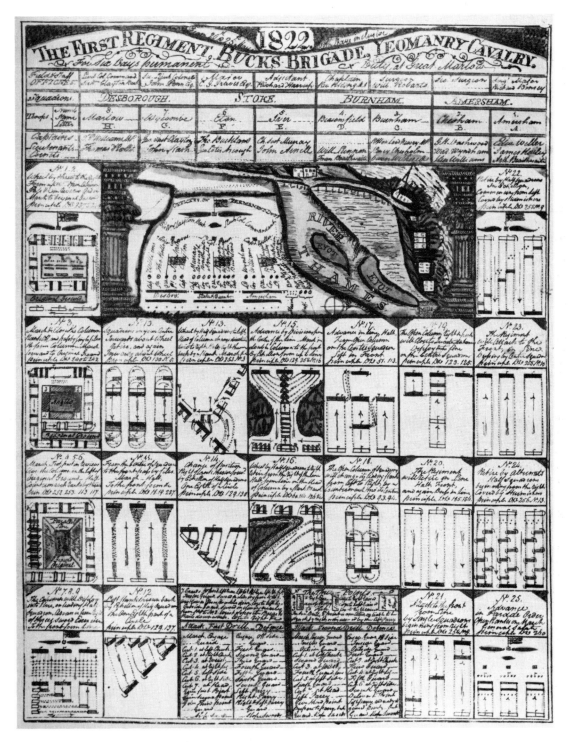

A hand coloured plan of the encampment of the 1st or Southern Regiment at Marlow during the permanent duty of May 1822. (CRO)

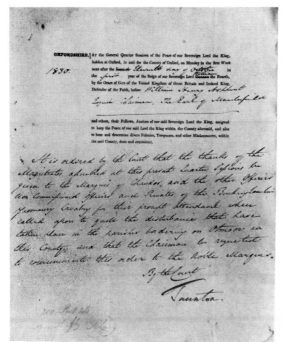

LEFT: The thanks of Oxfordshire Magistrates for the 2nd Regiment's services on Otmoor. (CRO)
RIGHT: Lancer's chapka of the Taplow Troop or South Bucks Yeomanry Cavalry.

BUCKS LIEUTENANCY.

Aylesbury, Dec. 2nd, 1852.

PRIVATE JOYCE,

I am directed by Lord Carington to inform you that his Lordship has received your Letter, acquainting him that the Sherrington Friendly Society, of which you are a Member, has refused you medical relief, in consequence of your having volunteered into the Militia. Lord Carington has forwarded your Letter to the Secretary of State, under whose consideration the question now is.

His Lordship understands you to have been a Member of this Society for two years, and to have paid a Monthly Subscription of One Shilling; he therefore desires me to send you a Post Office Order for Twenty-four Shillings, of which please to acknowledge the safe receipt.

Your humble Servant,
HENRY HEYWARD,
Clerk to the General Meetings.

To Private CHARLES JOYCE,
1st Company ROYAL BUCKS MILITIA, SHERRINGTON.

ABOVE: An Officer of the Artillery Troop of the 2nd Regiment, March 1844. First suggested in 1803, two six pounders were attached to the regiment in June 1820, two more being added after 1852. The troop formed part of the Buckingham Squadron until disbanded in 1876. (NAM) OPPOSITE BELOW: Radical opponents of the militia attempted to discourage militia recruitment by utilising long forgotten rules of the universally popular friendly societies, which often contained clauses excluding servicemen from benefits. Carrington reimbursed Bucks victims and was instrumental in having the law amended to prevent such victimisation of militiamen. (CRO)

ABOVE: Officers of the 2nd Regiment, 1844 showing (at left) morning dress and (at right) field dress. The unofficial title of 2nd or Hussar Regiment of Bucks Yeomanry Cavalry was borne from 1821 to 1845 although hussar dress was still worn after 1845, when as a result of the Queen's visit to Stowe the regiment became the 2nd Royal Bucks Regiment of Yeomanry Cavalry. (NAM)

Gentlemen vs. Players 1850-1899

By the 1840s there was growing public concern at the possibility of a French invasion attempt. Although in some ways irrational, such fears reflected French progress towards construction of the world's first ironclad fleet, and the frequent clash of Anglo-French interests. That in turn often provoked inflammatory language across the Channel. Most leading British soldiers were universally pessimistic about the outcome of any war, a leaked letter of the Duke of Wellington in January 1848 adding greatly to public fears. So, too, did the rise to prominence of Louis Napoleon, who became first president of the French 2nd Republic in 1848, and then Emperor, after a *coup d'etat* in December 1851. Thus Britain was to endure what were termed the 'Three Panics' of 1846-7, 1851-2, and 1858-9.

The first invasion scare of 1846 was of short duration, Lord John Russell's Local Militia proposals being shelved, only to be revived in February 1852 following Louis Napoleon's coup. This second bill also failed and brought down the government, but Lord Derby's new ministry entered office with a commitment to militia reform. Receiving the Royal assent in June 1852, the new Militia Act provided for the voluntary enlistment of 80,000 men in Britain, the (rather empty) threat of the ballot held in reserve. Quotas were again set according to population, with militiamen offered a £6 bounty in return for a commitment to five years' service and 21 days' (28 days from 1875) annual training — with the possibility of 56 days in a national emergency.

In the country generally recruitment was slow, the 2nd Lord Carrington spending most of the autumn of 1852 in the saddle in Bucks, while his recruiting agents also scoured the county. Traditional sources were tapped for recruits, but the healthy condition of the labour market hindered recruitment, with relatively high wages and a shortage of labour due to emigration and greater job mobility. Carrington's high standards also led to the rejection of many potential recruits, although the Royal Bucks remained highly dependent on labourers. Thus in both 1869 and 1886 training periods were to be postponed at busy times in the farming year. However, having recruited a regiment of high moral if not social quality, Carrington jealously protected it against attempts by the army to recruit militiamen during the Crimean War. In all, 61 battalions of militia were embodied, the Royal Bucks being on service from June 1854 to May 1856, with successive quarters at Weedon in Northants, Windsor, Canterbury, Woolwich and the Tower of London. At first it was judged illegal to recruit militiamen into the army, but manpower shortages compelled authorisation in November 1854. Carrington refused to co-operate, although eventually over 400 of the 1,723 men who passed through the Royal Bucks did go into the army. Carrington and other commanding officers rightly recognised that turning the militia into a conduit for the army would destroy its character. Regular recruitment from the militia was again discontinued in June 1860, but reinstated once more in May 1866. Thenceforth the militia became an adjunct to the army. Under the Localisation Scheme of 1873, militia (as well as volunteers) were linked with regular battalions in new sub-districts and, from 1881, under the Territorialisation Scheme, the militia became battalions of regular regiments. Thus, although it clung to the title of Royal Bucks King's Own Mililtia, the regiment was thereafter officially known as the 3rd Battalion, Oxfordshire Light Infantry.

Although favoured by most politicians, and by soldiers who realised they could not hope for a larger peacetime army, the militia did not satisfy the additional security needs offered by a revived volunteer corps. Some offers were accepted in 1852, but military objections to the gentlemanly corps envisaged prevented serious consideration until the 'third panic' of 1858-9. This arose from French reactions to an assassination attempt on Emperor Napoleon III by an Italian refugee named Orsini. He had close connections with fellow refugees in England, and a series of addresses to the Emperor from the French army implied a desire to follow 'wild beasts' to their 'dens'. Palmerston's attempt to placate the French, with a bill making it a felony to plot murder abroad, was regarded as meeting insult with concession, and his government fell. Once more Derby became prime minister at a time of crisis and, as France plunged into war with Austria-Hungary, the ministry reviewed defensive arrangements. Military opinion was no more favourable to volunteers than previously, but the government felt compelled to respond to a public mood well matched by the publication in *The Times* on 9 May 1859 of Tennyson's celebrated poem, 'The War', with its appeal of 'Riflemen Form'.

On 12 May 1859 a circular authorised the enrolment of volunteer corps; clearly the government felt this satisfied public opinion at no real cost, since units would be entirely self-sufficient. The terms of service were merely a selection from the clauses of the Yeomanry and Volunteer Consolidation Act of 1804 and, although a second circular on 25 May offered ammunition at cost price from government stores, it hardly revealed any copious concessions. However, the fall of Derby's minority government on other issues in June introduced a new element. On 1 July Palmerston's new government issued rifles, but largely as a lever over the infant volunteer force, with which it could swiftly be brought under central control. This was to be the pattern: increasing government expenditure requiring corresponding increases in efficiency and centralisation. Under a new Volunteer Act in 1863 a 20s capitation grant for efficiency was offered against attendance at nine drills per annum and an annual inspection. An additional 10s was available for extra efficiency. The basic grant was increased to 30s in 1869 and to 35s in 1887, while other allowances also increased, but efficiency requirements were progressively tightened too. For example, musketry standards were raised in 1869, 1887 and 1889. Such increasing commitment conflicted with the civil occupations of most of the new Rifle Volunteers.

The militia and yeomanry within Bucks were roughly analogous to the regular army in the country; they were equally drawn from relatively narrow social groups, unrepresentative of society as a whole. The rifle volunteers were specifically intended, according to the second circular of 25 May, 'to induce those classes to come forward as Volunteers who do not, under our present system, enter either the Regular Army or the Militia'. Since the militia largely drew its rank and file from labourers and the county's yeomanry from the farming community, this left the broad majority of the middling elements of society. The rules of the new corps formed in Bucks, as elsewhere, indicate at once the middle class idealism of the movement, with emphasis on honorary and enrolled members; entrance fees like that at Slough of half a guinea; annual subscriptions ranging from 10s at Winslow to half a guinea at Marlow; proposing and seconding of members; and discipline maintained by fines. Volunteers would provide all their own equipment, including uniform, which cost £3 at Aylesbury and £2 5s 0d at Marlow, where it could be paid off in instalments of 4s 0d per month. The character is best set by a circular at High Wycombe stating that 'It is the earnest wish of the Committee that the tone of the Corps should be that of gentlemen . . .'. In fact,

Bucks corps from the very beginning embraced a cross section of the community as a whole, corps being officially formed as the 1st Bucks (Marlow) RVC, (16 December 1859); 2nd Bucks (High Wycombe) RVC, (6 March 1860); 3rd Bucks (Buckingham and Winslow) RVC, (February 1860); 4th Bucks (Aylesbury) RVC, (11 May 1860); and 5th Bucks (Slough) RVC, (20 July 1860). Both the High Wycombe and Slough corps experienced early difficulties, the former through Carrington's attempt to manoeuvre his son into the command, and the latter through the departure of its first commanding officer, Lord Seymour, to fight for Garibaldi in Italy. Further projected corps at Amersham and Chesham, Newport Pagnell and Princes Risborough all failed to materialise.

The committee of the Aylesbury corps elected in December 1859 is broadly representative in its concentration of professional men — mainly solicitors, and tradesmen. Wherever possible, however, local gentry were sought as potential commanding officers, such as the Hon Percy Barrington and Thomas Fremantle to command the subdivisions at Buckingham and Winslow, and Sir Robert Harvey, who took over at Slough after Seymour's resignation. Barrington was to become first Lieutenant Colonel two years after the corps were brought into an administrative battalion in 1862. His successor was Charles Chester of Chicheley, whose family had a long record of local military service. Although by profession a brewer, Owen Wethered of Marlow, who succeeded Chester in command of the 1st Bucks Administrative Battalion, was also an Old Etonian. Wethered was adamant that the officers should remain gentlemen, responding to a suggestion by the 3rd Duke of Buckingham and Chandos in 1883 to promote some NCOs to vacancies, that 'I do not think it would answer to promote anyone who is not a gentleman by education and manners to our commissioned ranks'. The problem, as Wethered recognised, was that fewer gentlemen were available by 1883, for a perceptible change had come over the volunteer movement as early as 1862/1863. At first, as Wethered recorded of the Marlow corps, 'the officers were mortally afraid of offending their men — many of whom were of equal social standing with themselves'. Increasingly, however, professional men and even the tradesmen dropped out through want of enthusiasm, time or money, those remaining invariably becoming NCOs. Instead, the backbone of the rank and file became artisans, whom Wethered believed to be 'our natural recruiting ground as the agricultural and other day labourers are for the Regular Army and the Militia'. Successive commanding officers refused to recruit agricultural labourers, no one earning less than 18s a week regular wage being enrolled. In what was essentially an agricultural county this made the 1st Bucks Rifle Volunteers, as the battalion became on consolidation in 1875, dependent upon two principal sources. The first was the chairmakers of High Wycombe; a company was reformed there in 1875, after the original corps was disbanded four years earlier for indiscriminately firing ammunition after a field day in Burnham Beeches. The second was the employees at the carriage works of the London and North Western Railway at Wolverton, where a company was formed in October 1877. In 1897 the battalion was actually redistributed, to take account of the concentration of potential recruits at these two centres and when, in 1903, the battalion was offered a place in the so-called Field Army, Lieutenant Colonel Alfred Gilbey sought the prior permission of the Chairman of the LNWR before acceptance.

Civilian employment was of great importance, since the auxiliaries were clearly only temporary soldiers. Thus the first camp of the 1st Bucks Administrative Battalion at Marlow in 1865 was confined to only two full days 'as it was thought our men could not give more than that from their civil occupations'. But, at the same time, participation in the auxiliary forces also offered something to the employer, the belief growing in the 1850s that positive moral benefit was to be derived from the discipline inculcated in the militia and volunteers. The militia of 1852 has been characterised as a half-way house between a Sunday school and a superior mechanic's institute. Certainly Carrington introduced a regimental school and compulsory church attendance, as well as 'liberally providing them with Bibles and Prayer Books', while his successor, Walter Caulfield Pratt, urged his men after the annual training of 1868 to 'be careful to follow that mode of life which becomes the true Christian soldier'. Carrington had earlier in 1862 remarked that 'attention to orders, obedience to those in authority, temperance, honesty, industry and a desire to improve' would make militiamen 'respected, trusted and employed'. In the Wolverton Company of the 1st Bucks Rifle Volunteers, dismissal for indiscipline would also mean dismissal from employment with the LNWR. Such underlying social control also pervaded cadet battalions and other organised youth movements, such as the Boys Brigades that were to flourish in the 1880s.

Good discipline and conduct would also cement a working relationship between the civilian and those who temporarily donned uniform when auxiliaries were visible to society. In the Royal Bucks King's Own Militia there was great emphasis on good conduct during the annual training, the regiment receiving praise for its conduct at High Wycombe in 1862, 1864, 1866, and letters of appreciation from the town authorities in 1867, 1868 and 1869. Curiously, there were echoes of a more traditional apprehension of a military presence of any kind, when it was proposed to take the regiment to Aylesbury for the first time in 1887. Relationships were somewhat uneasy for several days but, in the end, some 506 leading citizens signed a memorial urging the regiment to return again. On two occasions the Bucks Volunteers upset the delicate balance between acceptance and hostility, and between respect and ridicule. In 1865, for example, the camp held by permission of the Parish Vestry on common land aroused 'a mob of indignant parishioners', who had to be driven off by the men drawing their bayonets: the mistake of using common land was not repeated. In October 1875 the regiment arrived late on a hot day at Stowe for a field day; a 'farewell entertainment' for the 3rd Duke of Buckingham and Chandos on his appointment as Governor of Madras. 'With empty stomachs and a consuming thirst', the men fell on what they thought was light claret and was, in reality, neat port. Marching down Stowe Avenue after the exercises had ended, so many men fell out that half the battalion was helping others along, with those totally incapable being conveyed to the station in farm wagons. As Wethered remarked 'we had made an exhibition of ourselves of a very disreputable character, and of course this was known throughout the county . . .'.

Yet, at the same time, the link between community and auxiliaries was such that the prestige of a whole or part of that community could feel slighted if the auxiliaries were done some apparent injustice. The town of High Wycombe greatly resented the disbanding of its volunteers in 1871, just as Slough resented the threatened disbandment of its volunteer band in 1869, for appearing at a political function in uniform and accepting money from the crowd. The interdependence of auxiliaries and local society included the ready cancellation of militia exercises in 1870 and 1871, for fear of spreading small pox prevalent at High Wycombe, and the need for the volunteers in particular to supplement grant income with public subscription. The Bucks County Rifle Association was launched on such subscription in 1863; in December 1889 a Bucks Volunteer Patriotic Fund was launched to raise £3,000, to equip the battalion in accordance with new mobilisation schedules, failure threatening forfeiture of the capitation grant. The other side of the coin, of course, was that the auxiliaries still generated trade. That was one reason for the reappraisal of the militia's presence at Aylesbury in 1887. The volunteers contracted out the provisioning of their annual camps between 1865 and 1875, while the 2nd Royal Bucks Regiment of Yeomanry Cavalry similarly contracted out its messing, usually to the landlord of the White Hart at Buckingham. However, on one occasion in 1872 the landlord had to be reminded that it was a condition of tenancy at the Duke's inns that horses were freely provided, to draw the regiment's artillery.

The unlimited opportunities for patronage inherent in auxiliary forces' trade should not be overlooked. When provisioning the militia in 1852, Carrington distributed purchases among eleven of High Wycombe's boot and shoemakers, five of fifteen butchers, three of twelve tailors and four out of six corn and flour dealers. Others to profit inlcuded beer sellers, victuallers and barbers, while anyone with the slightest connection to the militia felt themselves entitled to call upon Carrington for favours. Almost inevitably, local politics again became linked to auxiliary affairs. In 1864 Carrington as Lord Lieutenant passed over Sir Robert Harvey for command of the 1st Bucks Administrative Battalion, such appointments still resting with the Lieutenancy until 1871. Here was animosity, because Carrington had been unable to prevent Harvey becoming commanding officer of the Slough corps in 1860, for his men had petitioned for his appointment. More significantly, Harvey was newly elected as a Conservative MP and was also brother-in-law of the Duke of Buckingham and Chandos 'between whom and the Lord Lieutenant no love was lost'. Some years later, a Committee on the Yeomanry in 1875 recommended that all yeomanry should be light cavalry alone. The 2nd Royal Bucks appealed to the Prime Minister, Benjamin Disraeli, claiming that the loss of the regiment's artillery 'may produce, if carried out, a good deal of angry feeling among the farmers of the County hostile to the measures of the Government'. Disraeli did raise the matter with his Secretary of State for War, and the regiment was allowed to retain its two artillery troops, but not the guns, which were returned to store in early 1876.

The root of the friction between Grenvilles and Carringtons lay in the more recent arrival of the latter as Bucks landowners. Yet the auxiliaries as a whole performed a role in what might be termed social assimilation. Just as the rank and file might demonstrate a commitment to employer or landlord, so the commissioned ranks could provide an entrée to county society. In Bucks it is noticeable that the second, if not the first, generation of newcomers invariably sealed a commitment to the county by so serving. Egerton Hubbard, son of a Russian merchant elevated to the peerage as Lord Addington in 1887, had joined the 3rd Bucks RVC in 1863, and rose to command the 1st Bucks Rifle Volunteers from 1891 to 1900. The yeomanry performed a similar role, its connection with emerging Jewish families leading to the somewhat scurrilous nickname of the 'Flying Foreskins'. The chief beneficiaries of the sale of Grenville lands after the 2nd Duke's bankruptcy in 1848 were the Rothschilds. Nathaniel Mayer Rothschild, later 1st Lord Rothschild, entered the yeomanry in 1863. He was eventually promoted to Captain in 1885, 'in the interests of the regiment' since, although having little time for yeomanry duties, it was felt important that he did not lose interest. His son, Lionel Walter Rothschild, was a keen yeoman, entering the regiment in 1889, the year in which his father became Lord Lieutenant. Another new arrival quickly assimilated within the yeomanry was Harry W. Lawson, son of the 1st Lord Burnham, the family moving to Hall Barn in 1881, and Lawson being commissioned in the regiment in 1889, the year in which its title was changed to the Royal Buckinghamshire Hussar Yeomanry Cavalry.

Nevertheless, wealth alone would not confer acceptance in the yeomanry, as witnessed by the promotion of Lord Chesham, who had joined the yeomanry in 1879, to Lieutenant Colonel in 1889 only three months after his promotion to Major. Major James Poynter had no objections to Chesham's elevation since 'it is understood in a yeomanry regiment that a big man in the county will be promoted over less men and quite acquiesced in'. By contrast, another officer considered socially unsuitable for further promotion but senior in service to both Chesham and Poynter was persuaded to make way for them, by promotion to Major, on the strict understanding that he would retire one month later. In some counties, volunteer rank conferred few if any privileges, but in Bucks new men appeared to make no distinction between volunteers, militia and yeomanry. Indeed, many Bucks gentlemen held dual commissions in the auxiliaries, or passed through more than one branch. Walter Caulfield

Pratt served in both militia and volunteers, and Sir Robert Harvey served in both volunteers and yeomanry.

As a whole, the auxiliary forces undeniably projected military values to the public. It was true that they were few in number — militia, yeomanry and volunteers together represented only 3.6% of the male population in 1903. It was also true that the number of occasions when auxiliaries were seen in uniform was relatively limited — although even less was seen of regulars. But most, if not all, of the public could hardly be unaware of their existence. No formal county function was complete without them, much time and energy was devoted to their administration, much publicity was given in the local press to their activities. Through their disparate social composition, the auxiliaries also extended familiarity with military values throughout the whole community, involving many who would not otherwise have become involved in military affairs at all. In short, the auxiliaries were ever-present and played no small part in that growth of a more militarised society evident in late Victorian and Edwardian Britain.

To a large extent, the emphasis has been placed here on the social role of the auxiliary forces in the county but, of course, their primary *raison d'etre* was as military formations, that function becoming apparent once more as war broke out in South Africa.

ABOVE: Officers of the Royal Bucks King's Own Militia in the Orangery Cloister of Wycombe Abbey, 1855. Carrington maintained the social exclusivity of the officer corps, property qualifications still being required in any case until 1869. However, he also insisted on efficiency and combed out older veterans. (CRO) OPPOSITE: One of the recruiting posters 'well circulated about towns and villages' in 1852 for the newly revived militia, the county quota being set at 446 men based on the 1851 census. Some nine tenths of those recruited by November 1852 were labourers. (CRO)

KING·S OWN
REGIMENT,
ROYAL BUCKS
MILITIA.

NOTICE IS HEREBY GIVEN

(In compliance with the Statute 15th and 16th Victoria, c. 50),

That 446 able-bodied Men, resident in this County, between the ages of 18 and 35, desirous of enrolling themselves as VOLUNTEERS for the term of Five Years in the Militia of the County, are requested forthwith to deliver to the Constable of their Parish a statement of their names, residence, occupation, age, and height.

Every Volunteer will receive the sum of 10s. as a Bounty on Enrolment; and 10s. at the termination of the first training, if his conduct has been good: and, after that time, a further Bounty of 2s. a month, until he has received the full sum of £6. And these Bounties will be exclusive of the Pay during Training and Exercise.

Volunteers of 5 feet 4 inches may be accepted; and Men who have been discharged from the Army after three years' service, with a good character, will be accepted up to the age of 45.

Drummers will be accepted at 16 years of age, and under 5 feet 3 inches.

The Militia will be called out for Twenty-one days Training and Exercise in the month of October next.

By order of the Right Honourable the Lord Lieutenant of the County,

HENRY HEYWARD,

Clerk of the General Meetings of Lieutenancy.

Aylesbury, 2nd August, 1852.

G. CANNON, PRINTER, WYCOMBE.

ABOVE: Non-commissioned Officers of the RBKOM outside the Orderly Room in the Stableyard of Wycombe Abbey, 1855. Potential NCOs were also subject to close scrutiny. Thus, strenuous attempts were made in November 1856 to discourage an NCO marrying 'one of the commonest prostitutes of Wycombe'. (CRO) LEFT: Private Henry Lee of High Wycombe in the uniform of the RBKOM, circa 1863. (DP) RIGHT: Colonel Walter Caulfield Pratt of Oving House; formerly an officer in the 67th Foot, he joined the Royal Bucks in 1853, becoming Lieutenant Colonel in 1856, and Colonel 1868-1880. (CRO)

ABOVE: Three officers of the RBKOM, c1870. (AMOT) BELOW: Men of the RBKOM, now the 3rd Battalion, Oxfordshire Light Infantry, outside an Aylesbury public house during the annual training of May 1892. (CRO)

VALE OF AYLESBURY RIFLE CORPS.

At a Meeting held this 22nd Dec., 1859, at the County Hall, in Aylesbury, convened by Public notice,

It was Resolved—

That this Meeting considers it desirable that a Volunteer Rifle Corps should at once be formed for this Town and neighbourhood.

That the Corps shall consist of effective Members, who will be enrolled for active service, and will be subject to the regulations issued by the Secretary of State for War; and secondly, of Honorary Members, who will give a donation of two guineas, and an annual subscription of one guinea.

That a Committee be forthwith appointed for collecting donations and subscriptions, and

ABOVE: Resolutions passed at a meeting in Aylesbury, 22 December 1859, recommending the raising of a Rifle Volunteer Corps. One coal merchant voiced pacifist objections but the solicitor, Julian James, responded 'that if any gentleman was desirous . . . of having his nose pulled by a Frenchman, he must go to France and have it done, for they could not suffer it in Aylesbury market place'. (CRO) CENTRE: Boys of the Eton College RVC on the occasion of the presentation of a silver bugle by Lady Carrington, 22 November 1860. Always something of an anomaly, the corps was not officially named as the 8th Bucks RVC until 1867, becoming the 2nd Bucks (Eton College) Rifle Volunteers in 1878. (CRO) BELOW: The camp of the 1st Bucks Administrative Battalion at Stowe, 1-7 August 1872. (CRO)

Poster advertising the first field day of the infant Bucks Volunteers at Velvet Lawn, Chequers Court on 13 August 1860. Crowds of up to 8,000 reportedly watched the ladies of Aylesbury present a silver bugle to the 4th Bucks (Aylesbury) RVC. (MS)

ABOVE: Officers of the 1st Bucks Administrative Battalion in camp at Wakefield Lawn, Northamptonshire, June 1867. Included are Lt Colonel the Hon Percy Barrington (sitting, third left); the future Lt Colonels, Owen Wethered (standing, fourth left) and Lord Addington (sitting, first left); the well known publican, J. K. Fowler of the White Hart, Aylesbury (lying, front); and Sir Harry Verney MP (wearing top hat). (CRO) BELOW: The newly consolidated 1st Bucks Rifle Volunteers, showing signs of unreconciled uniform divergence, at Claydon House, August 1875. Sir Harry Verney, although aged 74, led the Eton boys (at rear) 'headers into the lake' while camped at Claydon. (CRO)

54

ABOVE: A group, mostly NCOs, of the 1st Bucks Rifle Volunteers in camp at Bourne End, August 1879. Close to the river, the camping ground was completely flooded by a storm necessitating a move to Wooburn. (CRO) BELOW: Boys of the 2nd Bucks (Eton College) Rifle Volunteers on the range, 1883. Apart from Eton, the boys of St Paul's College at Stony Stratford formed a cadet corps attached to the 1st Bucks from 1876 to 1883. At the latter the intention was to encourage boys to 'adopt the military profession'. (NAM)

ABOVE: One of a number of illustrations for a booklet on dress regulations in the 1st Bucks Rifle Volunteers, 1893. In theory the regiment had become the 3rd Volunteer Battalion, Oxfordshire Light Infantry in 1881 but refused either to adopt the title or the scarlet of the regulars and clung to the grey uniform. LEFT: A Trooper of the 2nd Royal Bucks Regiment of Yeomanry Cavalry, 1865; the earliest known photograph of the yeomanry, illustrating the smaller pattern shako adopted c1858 and the 1842 pattern musket-bore carbine (at rear). (AMOT) RIGHT: Richard, 3rd Duke of Buckingham and Chandos (1823-1889) and officers of the 2nd Royal Bucks Regiment of Yeomanry Cavalry at Stowe, 1878. (CRO)

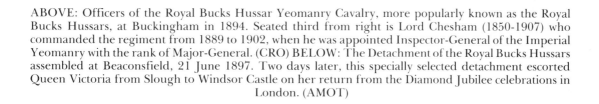

ABOVE: Officers of the Royal Bucks Hussar Yeomanry Cavalry, more popularly known as the Royal Bucks Hussars, at Buckingham in 1894. Seated third from right is Lord Chesham (1850-1907) who commanded the regiment from 1889 to 1902, when he was appointed Inspector-General of the Imperial Yeomanry with the rank of Major-General. (CRO) BELOW: The Detachment of the Royal Bucks Hussars assembled at Beaconsfield, 21 June 1897. Two days later, this specially selected detachment escorted Queen Victoria from Slough to Windsor Castle on her return from the Diamond Jubilee celebrations in London. (AMOT)

57

ABOVE: The Maxim Gun Detachment of the Royal Bucks Hussars at Stowe, c1900. The Royal Bucks was the first yeomanry regiment to possess a Maxim, the weapon presented by the Hon Lionel Walter Rothschild in 1897. (RR/H) BELOW: A group of NCOs and men of the Royal Bucks Hussars at Stowe, c1900. Seated centre, polishing boots, is Richard Roadnight, of Manor Farm, Chearsley. (RR/H)

Territorial Take-Over 1899-1914

At the close of the 19th century, many regular soldiers were still profoundly unimpressed by the military capability of the auxiliary forces. Nevertheless, real progress was made, not least by the auxiliaries themselves, to fit the auxiliaries for modern warfare as it then was. Both militia and volunteers had been brought into closer association with the army through localisation and territorialisation and, in the case of the volunteers and yeomanry, brigades were introduced in 1888/9 and 1893. The 1st Bucks Rifle Volunteers were thus placed in the Home Counties Volunteer Brigade and the Royal Bucks Hussars in the 2nd Yeomanry Brigade. Measures had also been undertaken by the auxiliaries to provide some of the absent previously supporting services, the 1st Bucks Rifle Volunteers adding a Bearer Company at Stony Stratford in 1880. Volunteers had also been given defined roles in the mobilisation schemes for home defence of 1875 and 1886, which was further modified after introduction of the brigade system.

However, there was a problem in actually employing auxiliary forces, even in home defence. Volunteers were only liable to be called out on 'actual or apprehended' invasion. It was not until 1895 that the government could accept offers of volunteer service upon the embodiment of the militia, such embodiment being deemed possible in the case of 'imminent national danger or emergency'. Enabling auxiliaries to serve overseas was even more problematical. Legislation in 1855 and 1858 had allowed offers of voluntary service from the militia, ten battalions serving in Mediterranean garrisons during the Crimean War. It was generally accepted, and confirmed by legislation in 1875, that such militia service could only be in garrison at Gibraltar, Malta or in the Channel Islands. Neither yeomanry nor volunteers could be used overseas at all, offers of service being rejected during the Eastern Crisis of 1878, which generally stimulated recruitment. In both 1882 and 1885 small specialist groups of volunteers were allowed to go to Egypt and Suakin on special attachment to the army, carrying automatic discharge at the end of the campaigns. Thus, when offers were renewed at the beginning of the South African War in October 1899, hasty provision was necessary to accommodate them.

It was not the government's original intention to accept such offers but policy changed as a result of the triple reverses at Magersfontein, Stormberg and Colenso in the 'Black Week' of 9-15 December 1899. A proposal by the Lord Mayor of London to raise what became the City Imperial Volunteers was accepted on 20 December. At the same time, in response to the request by Sir Redvers Buller for 8,000 Mounted Infantry after his defeat at Colenso, an Imperial Yeomanry Committee was established, and an appeal for volunteers made on 22 December. On 2 January 1900 the War Office also sanctioned the raising of 66 Active Service Companies from the volunteers, to be attached to regular battalions in South Africa on a year's engagement. Further calls were made for both service companies and the Imperial Yeomanry in January 1901 and January 1902. The militia was also embodied, with 68 battalions employed either in South Africa or Mediterranean garrisons.

In Bucks there was an enthusiastic response, not only among the traditional working class sources of recruits for militia and army, but among those middle class elements not glimpsed in the volunteers since the mid-1860s. Both the City Imperial Volunteers and the Imperial Yeomanry have, indeed, been characterised as 'structured for and by the middle classes', although there was an undoubted increase in the working class complement of the later contingents of the Imperial Yeomanry. In Bucks, reservists had joined the army at an early stage, those at High Wycombe leaving to scenes of patriotic fervour on 11 December 1899. There was also an immediate response to Lord Chesham's appeal for recruits for the Imperial Yeomanry. Two squadrons were to be raised for the 10th Battalion, IY under Chesham's command — the 37th Squadron at Buckingham under Captain W. de Winton, and the 38th at High Wycombe under Captain the Hon W. A. W. Lawson. The Royal Bucks Hussars had a Northants squadron from 1892 to 1902 and, apart from the yeomen themselves, the appeal attracted recruits in neighbouring counties as well. Two extant accounts are those of R. Spencer Britten, a farmer's son from Great Billing in Northants, and H. S. Gaskell, a medical student from Peterborough. Gaskell describes the recruits 'as the better sort of farmers, horse-dealers, etc, many of whom already belonged to the existing corps of Bucks Yeomanry, with one or two tradesmen and grooms, and a sprinkling of public school and University men'. The largest occupational group was indeed farmers, amounting to 25% of the 260 other ranks of the 37th and 38th Squadrons, with a similar percentage members of the Royal Bucks Hussars. Two further squadrons were subsequently raised in the county — the 56th and 57th Squadrons of the 15th Battalion — but they were socially far more diverse, and contained far fewer Bucks men.

The 1st Bucks Rifle Volunteers had to find approximately 60 men for the composite active service company to be attached to the 1st Battalion, Oxfordshire Light Infantry. The response varied considerably from company to company with, for example, 72 out of 151 men in the Wolverton Detachment volunteering for active service, and the remainder for garrison duty, while at Aylesbury only eight out of 40 volunteered for active service. In all, 70 men were selected for service under the command of Lieutenants C. A. Barron and L. C. Hawkins, the latter managing director of printers McCorquodale's of Wolverton. They embarked for South Africa on 10 March 1900, the 265 officers and men of the 37th and 38th Squadrons having gone a month earlier. The militia had already been embodied, and dispatched to garrison duty in Ireland.

By the time both yeomen and volunteers arrived in South Africa, the main Boer field army had been deefeated, and the British garrisons at Kimberley and Ladysmith, though not Mafeking, relieved. Despite the British successes, however, the war was to drag on for another two years, as a bitter guerrilla conflict was waged by Boer commandos. The Active Service Company was mostly employed in columns, sweeping the veldt clear of livestock, crops and Boer civilians, although there was one relatively static period spent around Heilbron from October to December 1900. There were many skirmishes, but few casualties other than those to disease. After a particularly rough passage out to South Arfica, the 10th Battalion, IY was employed with Lord Methuen's column doing 'all the advance guard and scouting work on trek'. A number of actions were fought, including that at Boshof on 5 April 1900, in which there were two notable deaths. The 37th Squadron lost Sergeant Patrick Campbell, husband of the celebrated actress, and the Boers lost the French Colonel, the Comte de Villebois-Mareuil. In a rather quixotic gesture, Chesham later had the heart and ceremonial trappings of the Frenchman's horse buried on the green at Latimer, above the memorial to 128 men of the village who served in South Africa.

For the Bucks servicemen in South Africa, particularly those in the Imperial Yeomanry, the tedious nature of war service on the veldt soon turned thoughts to home, although some men were induced to join the Free State Police. The remaining original members returned to Southampton on 16 June 1901, the active service company having preceded them on 17 May 1901. These and other returns generated a series of celebrations. At one level these were represented by the county reception for the Imperial Yeomanry at Daws Hill Park, High Wycombe on 17 June 1901, and by the reception for Lord Chesham at Buckingham on 25 July 1901. At another, there was the simpler but no less rapturous welcome given men when they returned to their own communities. Indeed the county community generally had supported its servicemen in innumerable ways. The Bucks County Fund had assisted in equipping the men in the first place, £3,047 3s 0d being raised for the Imperial Yeomanry, and £673 for the volunteers, by 4 January 1900. Then there were other local funds such as the 'Darktown Charity Organisation' at Wolverton, the *Buckingham Express* Relief Fund for the wives and families of North Bucks reservists, or village committees of the Transvaal War Fund, such as that at Whitchurch where 152 people had subscribed £11 0s 3d.

The war had also been marked by attempts to increase the strength and effectiveness of the county's auxiliaries, and particularly its volunteers. Emulating Middlesex, the Bucks County Council established a Home Defence Committee in January 1900. In March this recommended establishing a new central county range, promoting drill in schools, raising new rifle clubs, and adding three companies to the 1st Bucks Rifle Volunteers. The committee also wanted the government to authorise the raising of a new regular regiment for the county alone, W. W. Carlile MP raising the matter in the House. The County Rifle Association was reconstructed, and some rifle clubs did appear, such as that established at Iver by Tonman Mosley of Bangors Park, but the Secretary of State for War declined to receive a deputation on a county regiment.

Authority to augment the volunteers was one of a number of concessions made by the government, after its public acknowledgement in February 1900 that the volunteers were now the principal means of home defence, in the absence of army and militia. New powers were given to local authorities to acquire land for ranges, while legislation in August 1900 enabled the volunteers to be called out in Great Britain, in cases of 'imminent national danger or great emergency'. Camping allowances were also increased, and some battalions were able to attend month-long camps of emergency. But the government also intended to push up efficiency, even at the cost of reducing numbers, musketry standards being increased in December 1901 and annual camps made compulsory. This aroused opposition in many quarters, but the 1st Bucks accepted an invitation in August 1903 to join the Field Army scheme. This involved more training liabilities, including a thirteen day annual camp, exclusive of travelling. The yeomanry also experienced change, the entire force being re-equipped as mounted infantry in 1901, and its name changed to Imperial Yeomanry.

Of course, the shocks of a war so confidently undertaken, not least the eventual deployment of over 450,000 regular, auxiliary and colonial troops to defeat barely 50,000 Boers, was bound to provoke a reassessment of military policy. A series of official enquiries examined the consequences of defeat so narrowly avoided, and three successive Secretaries of State for War produced contrasting reform schemes. The plans of St John Brodrick, who occupied the War Office from 1900 to 1903, did not materially affect the auxiliary forces, beyond limited participation in his proposed six army corps and, in any case, he was unable to command sufficient political support for them. A Royal Commission on the militia and volunteers under the chairmanship of the Duke of Norfolk and appointed by Brodrick was still working when H.O. Arnold-Forster became Secretary of State. Its report, published in May 1904, concluded that neither force was capable of taking the field against continental regulars. Since the majority of the commissioners believed in the possibility of invasion, they therefore recommended replacing the auxiliaries with a home defence army raised by conscription.

Supporting the view of the Committee of Imperial Defence that invasion was impossible, Arnold-Forster totally rejected the report, and attempted to implement his own scheme. This aimed to create both a long and a short service army, existing simultaneously with an emasculated militia forming part of the short service army; the volunteers would be much reduced, and divided into two classes of efficiency. Concerted political opposition prevented any real progress, and it was left to the new Liberal Secretary of State, R. B. Haldane, to produce yet another reform scheme, after the Unionist government's defeat in the 1906 general election.

Haldane's scheme, of course, was to result in the creation of the Territorial Force, embracing both the yeomanry and the volunteers while, through its refusal to join either army or Territorials, the militia was abolished and replaced with the Special Reserve. It is important to emphasise, however, that the Territorial force as it emerged in April 1908 did not reflect the original conception of its architect. A number of crucial compr mises accompanied the evolution of the scheme between 1906 and 1907, to allay political opposition. Haldane projected the new administrative Territorial County Associations as unifying army and society — promoting military virtues among youth organisations and rifle clubs, and through a distinctive elective element provided by county and borough councils. The elective element was abandoned, and the powers of the associations curtailed, not least in their ability to promote cadet units. Similarly and of more importance, Haldane saw the Territorial Force as supporting and expanding his regular expeditionary force, with Territorials ready for overseas service after six months' continuous training upon mobilisation. Through fear of opposition, the Territorials were represented in 1908 as a means of purely domestic defence; those willing to commit themselves in advance to overseas service were later able to take the so-called Imperial Service Obligation.

1901 to 1908 was a period of considerable uncertainty for the auxiliary forces. In Bucks there was particular resentment at the prospect of losing the militia, the 3rd Battalion of the Oxfordshire Light Infantry (RBKOM) being finally disbanded on 31 July 1908, after a spirited campaign to save it. Frederick Verney MP had pushed Haldane to spare the battalion; there had also been an angry public meeting at Aylesbury on 14 January 1908, chaired by the Lord Lieutenant, Lord Rothschild. The very first resolution of the newly formed County Territorial Association, chaired by Tonman Mosley, on 10 January 1908, entered 'a most emphatic protest against the disbandment of the old and valued militia of which the County is so justly proud'. There was also alarm at the attempt to name the new Territorial infantry battalion the 5th Battalion, Oxfordshire Light Infantry. In the event, the pressure succeeded; not only was the new battalion to be known as the Buckinghamshire Battalion, but the regular regiment itself became the Oxfordshire and Buckinghamshire' Light Infantry.

There were also many problems in establishing the new units to be administered by the County Association. Generally, difficulties arose from the greater commitments required of Territorials than those required of the old yeomanry and volunteers. There was now to be a four year term of engagement with the right to resign on 14 days' notice (originally incorporated in volunteer legislation in 1804 and preserved in that of 1863) disappearing. There were to be more statutory drills and 15 days' annual camp, while renumeration was to be no more generous. Camps in particular were a problem, since so much depended upon the goodwill of employers. Bucks representatives were to press with others for separation allowances for married men and tax concessions for employers in such organisations as the Council of County Territorial Associations, and at meetings such as that at High Wycombe in November 1913 between the Association and the Director-General of the Territorial Force. Difficulties were experienced in taking over the property and buildings of some of the companies of the 1st Bucks Rifle Volunteers, and in promoting detachments in outlying rural areas. At Winslow, for example, men were wary of enlistment until travelling allowances were clarified; the decision to split the band into two contingents at Wolverton and High Wycombe adversely affected recruitment in Aylesbury. The creation of entirely new units also caused problems; the RAMC Mounted Field Ambulance at Stony Stratford and the Army Service Corps company at Taplow both drew recruits from other areas allocated to the Bucks Battalion, through higher pay and allegedly more attractive uniforms. The Bucks Battalion even considered a change to scarlet, but this was decisively rejected by the men, who remained much as before in terms of social composition: manual workers generally, and chairmakers and LNWR employees in particular. At Aylesbury there was also a steady increase in the number of printing workers entering the Bucks Battalion.

In the country as a whole, the initial good response to the creation of the Territorial Force faded as the invasion scare ended in 1909. The Territorials were also subjected to considerable criticism, both from the military authorities, who saw little point in expending limited resources on men not liable for overseas service, and from those advocating conscription as more appropriate to domestic defence. Criticism only generated more disillusionment, with numbers falling, particularly when the first four year term of engagement ended in 1912. By September 1913 the Territorial Force was over 66,000 men short of establishment, and barely 7% of officers and men had taken the Imperial Service Obligation. In Bucks, units had fallen to 83% of establishment by the eve of war from a peak of 93% in 1909, although this was far better than in many other counties. The Territorial Reserve established in 1910 was also a failure, with only one man and six officers enrolled in Bucks by 1914, although the so-called National Reserve was much healthier, and the county also had a small corps of Guides raised by Lieutenant Colonel W. J. Levi. An Officers Training Corps (Junior Division) had been formed at Wycombe Royal Grammar School, and cadet companies at Aylesbury Grammar School and Slough Secondary School but, although numbers were maintained, they were 'not increased'.

On the outbreak of the First World War, therefore, question marks hovered over the Territorial Force. It was one of the ironies of that war that, although the force was to more than prove its worth, its position was not materially improved.

The 3rd Battalion, Oxfordshire Light Infantry (RBKOM) leaving High Wycombe for garrison service in Ireland, January 1900. Embodied from 17 January to 7 November 1900, the battalion was stationed at Buttevant and Kilworth Camp in Co. Cork, whence over 200 men were drafted to units in South Africa. (BB)

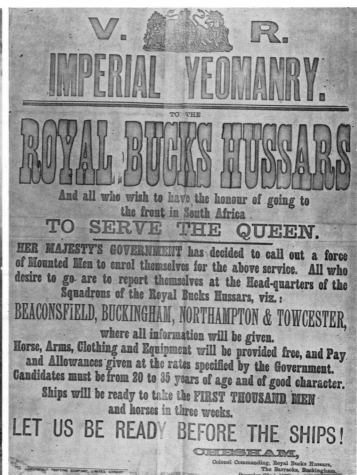

LEFT: Captain W. de Winton who commanded the 37th Squadron (Royal Bucks Hussars) of the 10th Battalion, Imperial Yeomanry in South Africa. Addressing his men at Buckingham, de Winton had said: 'I'll play up to you but, by Jove, you must play up to me as well. I want no rot'. (NAM) RIGHT: One of the recruiting posters for the Imperial Yeomanry widely circulated in Bucks and surrounding counties in December 1899. Lord Chesham set rigorous standards, testing claimed riding skills over hurdles at Buckingham where recruits were accommodated in the Town Hall. (CRO) OPPOSITE ABOVE: One of many celebrations for the return of contingents from South Africa: a reception in Aylesbury for Bucks men of the regular Oxfordshire Light Infantry, 16 October 1902; twenty four, excluding attached militia and volunteers, died on active service with the regiment. (CRO) BELOW: The unveiling of the South African War Memorial on Coombe Hill, 4 November 1904. First conceived in August 1901, it was erected on land donated by Bertram Frankland-Russell-Astley at a cost of £1,345 8s 9d, and contains names of 148 Bucks men who died in South Africa including 26 yeomen, 12 militiamen and 5 volunteers.

ACTIVE SERVICE VOLUNTEERS.

We sent to war from Aylesbury town,
    Four noble Volunteers,
Well drilled and trained by Sergeant Brown,
    Who here to-night appears.
I'll tell you once again their names,
    Although you know them all—
Bert Sirett, Fellows, Grimsdale, James,
    Obeyed the bugle call.

    And when the boys come back again,
        Ha ha! ha ha!
    We'll march to meet the railway train,
        Hurrah! hurrah!
    The band will play the NINETY FIVE,
        Old Aylesbury will be all alive,
    When the lads return from the war in Africa.

Yes, when the men come back again,
    We'll play the NINETY FIVE,
And march to meet the railway train
    To see them all arrive.
And if we were a borough town—
    Oh Aylesbury, what a pity!—
We'd give them, with a laurel crown,
    The freedom of the city!

We hope to hold two Big Bazaars,
    We mean to build a HALL,
Where Riflemen and Bucks Hussars
    Can drill, both great and small:
Then every kharki hero's name
    We'll carve in letters bold,
And hand their deeds to future fame,
    On brazen tablet told.

Another name, ah! mark it well,
    Cut deeper than the rest—
At Wepener young HORWOOD fell—
    He gave the QUEEN his best!
And yet another, far away,
    We won't forget to-night—
We won't forget Lieutenant Gray,
    May GOD defend the right!

LEFT: Verses written by Lance Corporal John Prothero for a volunteer dinner in Aylesbury in 1900 and re-issued in 1908 to stimulate Territorial recruiting. It commemorates Lt Horwood of the 1st Bucks, killed in action at Wepener in April 1900, and Lt Gray of the 1st OLI, who died shortly after his return from South Africa. (CRO) RIGHT: The new service dress adopted by the 1st Bucks Rifle Volunteers in April 1901 and personally approved by the Commander-in-Chief, Lord Roberts, when he inspected the battalion at Aldershot on 5 August 1901. There were apparently no regrets at the loss of the spiked helmet. (CRO) BELOW: 1st Bucks Rifle Volunteers at Addington Park, 22 June 1901. During the South African War attempts were made to recruit new companies at Chesham, Olney and Stony Stratford. In the event the only new company raised was at Bletchley, where it was maintained until the battalion reverted to an eight company establishment in 1908. (PS)

ABOVE: Lieutenant Coningsby Disraeli MP, and men of the 4th (High Wycombe) Squadron, Royal Bucks Hussars, 1903. Nephew of Lord Beaconsfield and heir to Hughenden Manor, Disraeli designed the regimental 'dizzie' consisting of a cooker with three cauldrons drawn by horses or mules, when on exercise with the regiment. (AMOT) BELOW: Drum banner of the Royal Bucks Hussars, or Royal Bucks Hussars Imperial Yeomanry as the regiment was formally known from 1901. It bears the new badge adopted in 1904 and the battle honour of 'South Africa' earned by the service of the 37th, 38th, 56th and 57th Squadrons of the Imperial Yeomanry for the regiment. (NAM)

1st Bucks Volunteer Rifles,

(Buckinghamshire Territorial Infantry.)

Wolverton Detachment.

In order that the conditions of transfer to, and service in, the new Territorial Army, may be fully understood by all concerned, the Detachment will Parade in Drill Order in the Large Hall of the Science and Art Institute, on Tuesday, 28th January, at 7.30 p.m., when the War Office Memo. on the subject, will be read and explained by the Commanding Officer, Lieut.-Colonel the Hon. T. F. Fremantle.

All N.-C. Officers and Riflemen of the Detachment are requested to attend.

Men who have served in this, or other Corps, and all young men of Wolverton, Stony Stratford, Stantonbury, and the district generally, are specially invited to be present.

It is hoped that in the New Buckinghamshire Territorial Infantry, the Wolverton Detachment may fully maintain its numbers and the reputation it has so long held in the 1st Bucks Volunteer Rifle Battalion, for smartness and efficiency.

H. M. WILLIAMS,
Major.

January 22nd, 1908.

ABOVE: The 1st Bucks Rifle Volunteers marching as part of the 23rd Field Army Brigade encamped at Sway in Hampshire in August 1905. Only 25 volunteer battalions were admitted to the Field Army scheme, the Bucks filling a vacancy in 1903. (CRO) LEFT: Poster advertising a public meeting at the Science and Art Institute, Wolverton on 5 February 1908 to explain to potential recruits the new Territorial Force. (CRO) RIGHT: Captain G. Christie-Miller and Major F. O. Wethered, Bucks Battalion, 1909. Christie-Miller affords a fine example of the dedicated amateur soldier in that he actually lived at Nantwich, but travelled regularly down from Stockport by train to attend on Wednesday evenings and at weekends while commanding the Aylesbury Company of the Bucks Battalion from 1907 to 1912. (CRO)

ABOVE: The South Midland Brigade Company, Army Service Corps, 1910. Raised from the cyclist sections of the 1st Bucks and 1st Berks Rifle Volunteers, the ASC should have confined its other recruitment to Taplow and Burnham but its novelty attracted men from other areas. Captain C. A. Barron had been with the Active Service Company in South Africa. (CRO) BELOW: Annual camp life in the Bucks Battalion of the South Midland Brigade, 1st South Midland Division of the Territorial Force: at Swanage in 1908. (CRO)

ABOVE and CENTRE: camp life again: church parade at Lulworth in 1911 and the cookhouse at the camp at Shorncliffe in 1913. Separation allowances were only made available to all married men for camps in 1912 and then only if they attended for the full fifteen days. The attitude of employers, particularly towards a second week, was also crucial. In this respect the LNWR was especially praiseworthy. (CRO) BELOW: One of an extensive series of numbered postcards of the Royal Bucks Hussars produced by the old established firm of L. Varney at Buckingham. This example shows the Maxim Gun Detachement at Stowe in 1912. Field service dress had been adopted in 1901.

ABOVE: A Detachment of the Royal Bucks Hussars in front of the statue of Lord Chesham unveiled in Aylesbury Market Place in 1910 by Field Marshal Lord Roberts, Chesham having died in a riding accident in 1907. Full dress uniform and the sword was, of course, retained after 1901 for ceremonial occasions. (BCM) BELOW: The Wendover Voluntary Aid Detachment, 1913. Administered by the County Territorial Associations, VADs would supply ambulance and nursing requirements in the event of war. By 1914 there were 28 detachments in Bucks with 788 men and women serving in them. (BCM)

ABOVE: The 1/1st Bucks Battalion leaving Aylesbury, 5 August 1914 for its first wartime station at Cosham, where three weeks were spent digging trenches for the defence of Portsmouth, prior to a week's training at Swindon. The men left according to the *Bucks Herald* to 'a roar of acclamation'. (CRO) BELOW: The 1/1st Bucks Battalion entering Chelmsford, 20 August 1914. Seven months were to be spent at Chelmsford, except two weeks' training under canvas at Great Totham in November 1914. (CRO)

Service Against Odds 1914-1918

Whatever the expectation of the Territorials on the approach of war in August 1914, all was to be set aside by the appointment of Lord Kitchener as Secretary of State for War on 5 August 1914. Kitchener's decision to ignore the County Territorial Associations as a means of expanding the army, and to raise his 'New Armies' instead, was understandable given the Territorials' pre-war failings; his precise reasons are still obscure. There were no actual plans for expansion through associations; perhaps it was thought they might be swamped by rapid augmentation of the army. Of course, the Territorials were not actually liable for overseas service unless they took the Imperial Service Obligation, while the recruits of the new armies were enlisted for general service from the start. Kitchener also appeared reluctant to pressure married men, as many Territorials were, into volunteering to go abroad. He was much preoccupied with invasion fears, against which the Territorials were supposedly the main defence. Yet the impression remains that his decision was an instinctive and immediate one for a regular soldier. Some Territorials were sent abroad in the autumn of 1914, principally to Egypt and India, but they were specifically to relieve regular garrisons for France, and Kitchener was only reluctantly persuaded to let Territorials go to France in the first winter of the war, to 'fill the gap' as casualties depleted the BEF.

In Bucks, the first duty of the County Territorial Association was naturally to mobilise its Territorial units. Almost immediately, a duplication was authorised, adding a 'second line' to the original 'first line'. Initially second line units were only raised where sufficient numbers in the first line had volunteered for overseas service, but a general duplication was ordered in September 1914. A 'third line' was then added from November 1914, where first line units had proceeded abroad, and for all counties from March 1915. The process of raising a 2/1st Royal Bucks Hussars and a 2/1st Bucks Battalion, as the second line units were designated, went reasonably smoothly, as did the creation of a 3/1st Royal Bucks Hussars and a 3/1st Bucks Battalion. Some pride was taken in the unequal comparison made between the uniform and equipment of the 2/1st Bucks Battalion and the plain clothes and dummy rifles of local 'Kitchener' recruits. However, there was undeniable competition in recruitment between Territorials and the New Armies. The Association was later to complain about this, although it offered alternative accommodation for Kitchener recruits, when the Oxford depôt of the Oxfordshire and Buckinghamshire Light Infantry became overcrowded in early September 1914. It was also a matter of Association policy that no pressure should be applied to recruits to join either the Territorials or the regulars when they presented themselves at recruiting offices. As a result, by 20 June 1915, the Association had found 3,291 men for the Territorials and 2,640 for the New Armies.

Nevertheless, unnecessary duplication of effort damaged both Territorials and the New Armies countrywide, although there were certainly legislative difficulties, of which Kitchener was well aware, in actually employing the Territorials abroad. The tragedy was that these difficulties were so approached by the military authorities that the Territorials emerged from the First World War with a deepfelt sense of grievance. One difficulty, for example, was the question of the Imperial Service Obligation. Prior to August 1914, an invitation was extended to units to volunteer for overseas service. Many pre-war Territorials were older, or had more family responsibilities than newer wartime recruits. Still others were too young for overseas service, enlistment in the Territorials being possible at 17, but overseas service not permitted until the age of 19, and yet others were physically unfit for active service. When the 1/1st Bucks Battalion was requested to volunteer at Chelmsford on 11 August, only 553 men initially did so, although the number rose to 600 the following day. Those opting for home service, including many older NCOs and all 27 members of the band, amounted to about 240. They were deprived of their equipment and made to camp apart from the rest of the battalion, then sent to dig trenches before being returned to the 2/1st Bucks. In the words of one officer of the 2/1st, they had not been 'treated by either officers or men in the manner contemplated by the King's Regulations'. Not surprisingly, there was antipathy between the two battalions thereafter, which persisted even after the war, separate Old Comrades' Associations being established and even separate war memorials in St Mary's Church at Aylesbury.

Matters were not improved by the subsequent refusal of the 2/1st Bucks Battalion to send their most experienced officers and NCOs to the first line when the latter went overseas in March 1915. When the 2/1st, in turn, was requested to volunteer for service, the greater understanding borne of experience brought far higher acceptance, including all but one member of the band who had refused to go with the 1/1st Bucks. However, there were still some 140 men, mostly elderly or unfit, but including some 'not pressed' by their officers to volunteer, who were returned to the 3/1st Bucks Battalion. The less desirable men were then promptly sent back to the 2/1st in the first reinforcing draft received from the 3/1st Battalion! By comparison, the Royal Bucks Hussars had few problems. F. H. Cripps, son of the 1st Lord Parmoor, who commanded a squadron in the 1/1st Royal Bucks Hussars, later recalled that he had asked any men not wishing to volunteer, to rein back two horses' length while drawn up in front of a wall. 'Obviously, no one was able to do so even if they had been so inclined. I was, therefore, able to inform my commanding officer that 100 per cent of the men under my command had volunteered for service abroad.' According to Cripps, only two men subsequently withdrew. Yet there was still some animosity between officers and men of the 1/1st and 2/1st Royal Bucks Hussars due to seniority problems, when the latter were drafted to the former during the war.

Related to the Imperial Service Obligation was the ability of the Territorials to enlist for home service only until as late as March 1915. It was not until the introduction of conscription, under the Military Service Acts 1916, that this and the ability of pre-war Territorials to seek their discharge at the end of the four year term of engagement (automatically extended by one year in war) were finally rescinded. There are examples of men declining to re-enlist and going home time-expired in both 1/1st Royal Bucks Hussars and 1/1st Bucks Battalion. In the case of the former, for example, Frederick Lawson complained in February 1916 that men aged 24-25 were going home time-expired from his squadron, drawn by tales of 'enormous wages to be gained and the soft jobs to be got at home'. In the 1/1st Bucks Battalion some 91 men went home time-expired between March 1915, when the battalion reached France, and the cessation of the concession a year later. A further 33 re-enlisted in the same period, while 26 men were subsequently compulsorily retained in the service after the introduction of conscription.

An even greater difficulty was the theoretical illegality of transferring Territorials between units, even within the Territorial Force, or of disbandment or amalgamation of Territorial units. It became all but impossible to maintain the 'territorial' integrity of the force, with the drafting system breaking down at an early stage. The degree of change in the Bucks Battalions may be seen in the percentage of men killed or died on active service, who were either born in, or resided in, Bucks parishes. In the 1/1st Bucks, 65% of the battalion's dead in 1915 were from Bucks parishes and 70% in 1916, but only 34% in 1917 and 38% in 1918. The figures for the 2/1st Bucks Battalion are 68%, 43% and 45% for 1916, 1917 and 1918. Inevitably casualties had an impact on the composition of the battalions, the majority of the wartime casualties for both units occuring within short periods of active operations.

The 1/1st Bucks Battalion, for example, suffered 242 casualties around Ovillers and Pozières on the Somme, between 21 and 24 July 1916; its next significant casualties occured on 16 August 1917, when 291 were suffered around St Julien, during the 3rd Ypres operations. Similarly, the 2/1st Bucks suffered 322 casualties in its first major action near Laventie on the Somme on 18/19 July 1916, within three months of arrival in France. The second significant action near Wieltje during the 3rd Ypres campaign on 22 August 1917 cost 349 casualties. After the Somme, the 1/1st Bucks received its first draft of 'strangers' from the 1/1st Hunts Cyclists while, after St Julien, a large draft was received from the Army Service Corps (Motor Transport). Similarly, the 2/1st Bucks received large drafts from northern Territorial battalions after the Somme. As these men had volunteered for service on the understanding that they would serve with northern units, they reached the 2/1st Bucks in 'bad humour' which, coupled with the receipt of officers from four different regiments, gave the 2/1st a 'rocky time'. In the 1/1st Bucks, only two of those officers who had landed in France in March 1915 served continuously with the battalion throughout the war with, in all, 142 officers passing through it — over four times the establishment.

The 1/1st and 2/1st Royal Bucks Hussars were, by contrast, more cosmopolitan from the beginning. Through the Rothschild connection (Evelyn and Anthony de Rothschild served with the 1/1st) a number of officers and men linked to the Newmarket racing fraternity entered the regiment. Similarly, through the Lawsons, employees of the *Daily Telegraph* were recruited and, uniquely, there were Lawsons commanding both 2/1st and 3/1st Royal Bucks Hussars, while a third served in the 1/1st Royal Bucks Hussars — Colonel the Hon H. L. W. Lawson, former commanding officer of the Royal Bucks Hussars, commanded the 3/1st during the war; his brother, Lt Colonel the Hon W. A. W. Lawson, commanded the 2/1st; and E. F. Lawson, son of W. A. W. Lawson, served with the 1/1st Royal Bucks Hussars before later commanding the Middlesex Yeomanry. The Royal Bucks Hussars had London recruiting offices both in Henry Street and, later, in St Swithin's Lane and, in addition to the Newmarket and *Daily Telegraph* contingents, large numbers of London policemen were also recruited.

The quality of drafts undoubtedly declined during the course of the war. First so-called 'Derbyites' were received, then middle-aged conscripts and, finally, 18-year-olds, all increasingly lacking in intelligence, physique and discipline. The arrival of the draft from the ASC brought a major increase in crime to the 1/1st Bucks Battalion. Indeed, newcomers after July 1917 accounted for 33.8% of all crime recorded for the battalion throughout the entire war. The letter books of Lt Colonel L. L. C. Reynolds, who commanded the 1/1st Bucks from 1916 until 1922, reveal a succession of unsuitable young officers. Some drafts reaching the 1/1st Royal Bucks Hussars later in the war could not ride. Not surprisingly, the question of drafting was a major issue for Territorial representatives in Parliament, compelling the War Office to issue a detailed defence in February 1919, stressing that military necessity had to prevail. That was, of course, reasonable, but it was viewed in the light of other grievances. Throughout the war, for example, Territorials complained that regular officers frequently adopted, at best, a patronising attitude, if not one of outright hostility. Few Territorials rose above the rank of Lieutenant Colonel, or held more than lowly positions on divisional staffs. In the 2/1st Bucks it was believed that the failure of their first attack was used as an excuse to remove the last remaining Territorials from brigade and divisional appointments, while the regular staff of the 61st Division were said to have 'gloried in their contempt' for the Territorials under their command. It is clear that regulars generally appear to have expected little of the Territorials, and failed to understand either their problems or the peculiar 'family atmosphere' of Territorial formations, where discipline was less rigid.

Yet a further cause for complaint was the steady erosion of County Territorial Associations' powers. At first, there had been much to do, not least in recruitment, since it is now apparent that the popular concept of a 'rush to the colours' in 1914 needs serious revision. By November 1914 the flow of recruits at Oxford had already dropped from 200 to 25 a day. The Bucks Association briefly considered attempting to raise a new and separate Bucks regiment to stimulate recruitment, but decided against it. The county's Recruiting Committee calculated in January 1915 that only five per cent of the total male population and only 20% of those realistically eligible for service had so far enlisted, but that the limit of voluntary effort had probably been reached. A number of new ventures were attempted, such as marching a 'smart detachment' through the county in May 1915, but in August it was resolved to discontinue public meetings since they no longer attracted eligible men. The solution, it was thought, was to visit men in their homes. A vigorous house-to-house visitation had begun in November 1914, and was supplemented from May 1915 with window badges. The personal approach was also the basis for the nationwide Derby Scheme from October to December 1915. In effect this was a canvass of men's willingness to enlist if called upon to do so, but with the proviso that single men would be called first. The scheme was carried out by local political parties, the Mid-Bucks area being organised by the Liberal agent, Edward Lacey. In Lacey's returns some 46% of those canvassed enlisted or promised to do so, while 28% could claim exemption and 26% declined absolutely. Disappointing results over the country as a whole sounded the death knell of voluntary enlistment, so conscription for single men aged 18 to 41 was introduced in January 1916 and, after criticism that the pledge to call on all single men first was not being observed, conscription for all males aged 18-41 came into effect in May 1916. Subsequently, the age limit was raised to 50 in April 1918.

With the introduction of conscription, the duties of the County Territorial Association changed, since responsibility for recruiting was taken over by the War Office. The Association's task became one of attempting to ensure that Bucks men still reached Bucks units, a task in which the Association was reduced to virtual impotence, as Territorial Association statutory powers were whittled away. It was only concerted action by the Council of County Territorial Associations that prevented the closure of Territorial depôts between September 1917 and January 1918. The Bucks Association complained at rumours of battlefield amalgamations in the Territorial Force in April 1916 while, in October, it complained that an attempt was being made to foist Oxfordshire and Buckinghamshire Light Infantry badges on the 3/1st Bucks Battalion. In October 1917 it fought against the closure of the Bucks depôt in Aylesbury and, following the disbandment of the 2/1st Bucks Battalion in the reductions consequent on the manpower shortages of early 1918, managed to extract a promise from the Adjutant General that the 1/1st Bucks would not suffer the same fate. By 1919 it was demanding a separate county regiment, and an official letter recognising the services of the 2/1st Bucks Battalion, which had, of course, been raised and equipped entirely by the Association. The Association did its best to ensure the continuing welfare of its servicemen, including prisoners of war, and in paying separation allowances to wives and dependants. Although its former recruiting officer, Captain L. H. Green, was now employed by the War Office, he still made regular reports to the Association on the results of tribunals held under the Military Service legislation. In Bucks, as elsewhere, there was surprising disparity between tribunals, in the attitudes taken towards appeals against conscription. Between January and April 1917, for example, the percentage of cases dismissed varied from 3½ at High Wycombe to 45 at Marlow, with an average rejection rate of appeals across the 22 tribunals in the county of 19.4. But then, Britain generally applied conscription with remarkable tolerance, compared to other belligerents.

About the only additional responsibility assumed by County Associations was the generally unpopular administration of the newly revived Volunteer Force in 1916. Both volunteers and the Special Constabulary were a response to continuing fears of invasion. The official scale of possible attack by the Germans against the east coast was not significantly reduced until December 1917. The Special Constabulary, numbering 4,120 by 23 September 1914 in 31 companies in the county, wore no uniform, but carried a warrant card and a truncheon or night stick. They were theoretically responsible for guarding key points against sabotage while, in the event of invasion, they had duties in handling refugees expected from eastern counties, and for the evacuation of livestock. Under plans laid from October 1914, a Bucks Central Organising Committee and a series of Local Emergency Committees earmarked sites for 'concentration' or rest camps for refugees, and for the collection of vehicles and livestock. In the northern division, for example, livestock would have been collected at Hanslope Park, Whaddon Park and Olney Park Farm, while refugees would have been accommodated in camps at Bury Field, Newport Pagnell, and at Woughton Green. Clergymen and girl guides were allocated to assist at the camps under police supervision.

The new volunteers, or Volunteer Training Corps as they were originally known, owed much to the sponsorship of Lord Desborough of Taplow and the Marquis of Lincolnshire of Wycombe Abbey. As W. H. Grenfell, Desborough had served in the 1st Bucks Volunteers, while Lincolnshire, as 3rd Lord Carrington, had commanded the RBKOM from 1881 to 1886, becoming Lord Lieutenant on the death of Lord Rothschild in 1915. Almost as soon as the war began, unofficial and illegal town or civic 'guards' had appeared, including such groups at Eton, Taplow and High Wycombe. Rather more formally, a prominent Liberal member of the London County Council, Percy Harris, suggested a 'London Defence Force' on 6 August 1914. This attracted considerable support, including that of Desborough, who became president of an interim committee. The committee was authorised by the War Office on 4 September 1914 to instruct Londoners not of military age in drill and musketry. So many enquiries were received that the committee transformed itself into a Central Association of Volunteer Training Corps. Official sanction was received on 19 November 1914, provided no conventional military ranks were used, or military uniform (beyond an armlet) worn.

Through the initiative of Lincolnshire, a short bill was prepared to regulate the VTC but, when this ran out of parliamentary time, it was decided in May 1916 to apply the provisions of the 1863 Volunteer Act, which had not been removed from the statute book by the Territorial and Reserve Forces Act of 1907. The Central Association now became one of Volunteer Regiments, with administration devolved to County Territorial Associations in September 1916. With the introduction of conscription, tribunals were empowered to exempt men from military service, provided they joined the volunteers but, under the 1863 Act, such men could resign after giving 14 days' notice. As a result, a new Volunteer Act was passed in December 1916, compelling all to serve for the duration and to undertake statutory drills. Six distinct categories were introduced, with some entitled to a capitation grant of £2, but this rarely proved sufficient, and additional funds were sought from local authorities. In Bucks, funds had been contributed by many prominent individuals, including Lord Rothschild and Waldorf Astor, who gave 2,000 Snider and Martini rifles between them, but the approach to local councils was less satisfactory: Chesham Urban District Council refused to give any money at all.

Three volunteer battalions had originally been envisaged in Bucks: the 1st or Southern based on Slough, Gerrards Cross and High Wycombe; the 2nd or Mid Bucks based on Aylesbury, Chesham, Princes Risborough and Wendover, and a 3rd or Northern centred on Bletchley, Newport Pagnell, Stony Stratford and Wolverton. In April 1915 it was decided to form a 4th Battalion, taking in High Wycombe, Gerrards Cross, Marlow and the Chalfonts, while the 1st Battalion centred on Eton, Slough, Burnham, Taplow and Wooburn. By November 1915 there were 2,751 volunteers in the county. In terms of previous service, age and social composition, some 18% of the 2nd Battalion between February and August 1915 had previous military experience of some kind while, in the 3rd Battalion, almost 40% between July and December 1916 were either under or over military age, with an equal percentage manual workers. Subsequently, the 4th Battalion was amalgamated with the 1st, when volunteer numbers were officially reduced in early 1918, and in July 1918 the 1st, 2nd and 3rd Battalions became the 3rd, 4th and 5th Volunteer Battalions of the Oxfordshire and Buckinghamshire Light Infantry.

The significance of the age figures of the 3rd Battalion in 1916 lies in the fact that the majority of the men were of military age; either those protected from military service by way of reserved occupation, or men sent by tribunals. The arrival of the latter category in 1916 was held to have changed the whole nature of the volunteers, since they formed an increasingly large proportion of the force. By January 1917 almost half the 2nd Battalion were 'tribunal men' — and well over half the 3rd Battalion. From the volunteers' viewpoint this was highly unsatisfactory, since many tribunal men proved unwilling or unable to complete even the minimum statutory drills, and the tribunals often appeared unhelpful in compelling them. The tribunal at Chesham proved particularly difficult; with the attitude of the Urban District Council this was damning, for 'when these two representative bodies both slight the Force, the rest of the town naturally takes little interest'.

Further difficulties were experienced with the scattered nature of the companies in a rural county, the Wing Company of the 2nd Battalion alone having detachments ten to twelve miles apart. Its commanding officer, Captain J. Tarver, reported in July 1916 that he feared 'there must always be . . . about one third of the strength behind the others in general efficiency'. Similarly, the acting adjutant, R. J. Thomas, the county surveyor, responded to a suggestion of increased drills in October 1916: 'A farm labourer working seven days a week from early morning until late in the evening could not possibly attend four or five nights a week nor could efficient instructors *unpaid* be found to drill them'. Indeed, in 1917 a general concession was made to 'agriculturalists' in the Volunteer Force, exempting them from half the specified drills between July and September. Notwithstanding the problems, the volunteers performed some useful tasks, such as digging the London defences and moving munitions. In Bucks they undertook guard duties on railways, wagons on railway sidings, and guarded prisoners-of-war cutting wood. They also manned night observation posts for Zeppelins and, despite the difficult time of year, responded well to the government appeal for active service companies to relieve regular troops on coastal duties, when all available men were required in France, following the German spring offensives of 1918. Five officers and 63 men of the Bucks Volunteers thus relieved the 2/25th London regiment from duty at Wickham Market in Suffolk from 29 June to 28 September 1918. In all, over 13,000 volunteers performed such duty in the same period.

During the First World War, some 19,450 Bucks men joined the armed forces prior to the introduction of conscription, their names being inscribed on a roll of honour at the suggestion of the Chairman of the County Territorial Association, Tonman Mosley (who was elevated to the peerage as Lord Anslow for his services). In accepting the roll in January 1918, the Lord Lieutenant, the Marquis of Lincolnshire, reminded his audience that there were also some 3,000 volunteers, 4,000 Special Constables and all those who worked on the land or in local industries who had equally played their part. The response from a county with a total population of only 219,000 (in 1911) was impressive even if, in the last analysis, the numbers were less than a single days' casualties on the Somme. There is little doubt that the county's units acquitted themselves well — the 1/1st Royal Bucks Hussars at Gallipoli, in the western desert, in Palestine and France; the 1/1st Bucks Battalion in France and Italy; the 2/1st Bucks Battalion in France; and the 2nd South Midland Mounted Brigade Field Ambulance at Gallipoli, in the western desert, Palestine and Syria. In all, Bucks units (excluding the Field Ambulance) recorded 1,014 deaths from all causes among officers and other ranks. Not all were Bucks men but, equally, many Buckinghamshire men died on active service with other units too.

The reward afforded the Territorial Force for its efforts and sacrifice was minimal, Territorial disembodiment commencing in December 1918. Thoughts on terminating the services of the volunteers had begun even earlier, although the Volunteer Act was not formally suspended until November 1918, with the force put into suspended animation in February 1919, and disbanded from September 1919. However, the Motor Volunteer Corps, in 28 counties including Bucks, were kept in being until March 1921 for their potential in aid of the civil power during strikes. Prior to the cessation of direct voluntary enlistment, some 725,842 had enlisted in the Territorial Force, or approximately half the number who had enlisted in the New Armies. But it must be borne in mind that the ability of the Territorials to recruit had been restricted by official policy and, imperfect though it may have been as a means of expansion, the Territorial Force still made a major contribution to the war effort. That its reward fell so short was regrettable, but merely a reflection of the traditional fate of the auxiliary military forces in Britain.

D (Wolverton and High Wycombe) Company, 1/1st Bucks Battalion marching to church parade at Chelmsford on the first Sunday after their arrival, August 1914. The battalion was billeted in large premises such as the prison and in private homes. (BMT)

ABOVE: Christmas Dinner for the 1/1st Bucks Battalion at Chelmsford, December 1914. A cause of resentment among Territorials was the cancellation of their leave because of an invasion scare while men of the New Armies received Christmas leave. (BMT) BELOW: The 1/1st Bucks Battalion leaving Chelmsford for the front, 30 March 1915. The battalion was followed at Chelmsford by the 2/1st Bucks Battalion, an officer of the latter writing of the inhabitants, 'They were sick of the 1st Bucks and were, before the end of our time, sick of the 2nd Bucks.' (CRO)

ABOVE: An early photograph of the 1/1st Bucks Battalion in France, probably in the Ploegsteert sector between 15 and 27 June 1915 judging from 'Messines' inscribed on the back and the evidence of trees in the background. It was the first tour of duty following training with units of the 4th Division in the trenches. (BBO) BELOW: Two photographs of the 1/1st Bucks Battalion, probably taken shortly after arrival in the Hébuterne sector south of Arras where trenches were taken over from the French in July 1915. The battalion and the division remained in this sector until July 1916. (BBO)

LEFT: Y Sap at Hébuterne facing towards Gommecourt Wood in the bitter winter of 1915/16. The sentry of the 1/1st Bucks Battalion marked is Private Lovell while the NCO wearing the cape is Sgt Smewin of No 4 Platoon. The trenches repeatedly collapsed in the winter weather. (BBO) RIGHT: Extract from the Trench Log for the 'Right Company, Left Battalion' in the Hébuterne Sector, Christmas Day, 1915 when C Company of the 1/1st Bucks Battalion was on duty. Despite the absence of truce on this day, it was recognised as a 'quiet' sector of line. (CRO) BELOW: The attack of the 1/1st Bucks Battalion between Ovillers and Pozières, 23 July 1916 by W. B. Wollen. From the relative peace of Hébuterne, the battalion moved to active operations on the Somme, a series of attacks from 20 to 23 July costing dear. (NAM)

LEFT: Captain E. V. Birchall, 1/1st Bucks Battalion. Within hours of writing a letter of condolence to Lionel Crouch's parents, Birchall was himself mortally wounded on 23 July 1916 leading D Company. He left a legacy of £2,000 for the welfare of the battalion's widows and orphans when he died of his wounds on 10 August 1916. (CRO) RIGHT: Lieutenant Oscar Viney, 1/1st Bucks Battalion, had only rejoined the battalion, which he was to command from 1930 to 1934, on 20 July 1916 before being seriously wounded three days later. (CRO) BELOW: B Company, 1/1st Bucks Battalion in training behind the lines at Forceville near Oisemont between 9 and 29 January 1917. After absorbing drafts the battalion had spent a trying period in the Le Sars sector at the end of 1916. It was the pulled out for further rest and training. (CRO)

"SOMME—B"HOYS" 1ST. BUCKS.

D. Coy. Sgts. Mess	Account.				
	Fr.	cts.	On. Service July 1916	Fr.	cts.
Subscriptions.			Expenditure		
Cash in Hand	1	50	8 Lines of Sausages	9	40
C.S.M. Read. R.	6	50	16 Tins of Fruit	32	00
C.Q.M.S. Jolliff. B.	6	50	7 Bottles of Sauce	8	90
Sgt. Barrett F.B.	6	50	Cake	5	00
" Fowler C.	6	50	Salad	1	30
" Mines A.y.	6	50	Papers. etc	2	40
" Franklin A.	6	50	Eggs.	7	00
" Williams. J.	6	50	Cooks & Waiters	10	00
" Walduck L.a.	6	50	Balance in Hand.	2	00
" Brooks. L.	6	00			
" Buss P.a.	6	50			
" Price R.	6	50			
" Brookes. A.	2	00			
" Bridgett. J.	3	00			
	78	00		78	00
July 16th Cash in Hand	2	00	Jno. Dell		

1ST BUCKS BATT.

BEER COMPANY.

1917.　　　## MENU.　　　1917.

BUON　　　　　　　　　　　　NATALE

JIPPO.

ROASTIO TURKIO.　　HAMIO.　　ROASTIO BEEFIO.

PULVERISED POMMES.　　LEGUMES.

(BARRAGE LIFTS AFTER 3 MINS)

PUDDEN NATALE.

H & Ps & STAND AT EASE.　　　　COFFEE & S.R.D.

VINO ITALIANO.

KNUTS.　　　ACQUA.　　　ORANGIOS.

SONGS.　YARNS.　　BON SANTES.　WIND UP.

TOM SMITH'S No. 5s.

OPPOSITE ABOVE: Men of the 1/1st Bucks Battalion's B Company wounded during the Somme operations on convalesence at Bedford House, Cheltenham, 1916. Seated second left is Private W. Baldock, who was to win the MM in 1917. In all, the battalion had 611 casualties on the Somme. (BMT) BELOW: In the midst of war life goes on — the account book of the Sergeants Mess of D Company, 1/1st Bucks Battalion for 4-15 July 1916, kept by CQMS B. Jolliffe. (BBO) ABOVE: A 'Menu Card' of B Company, 1/1st Bucks Battalion, Santa Croce Bigolina, Italy, December 1917. Following active operations in the Ypres Salient, the 48th Division was moved to Italy in November 1917. (BMT) BELOW: Captain Guy Crouch of B Company, 1/1st Bucks Battalion with others in Italy. A solicitor like his elder brother, Lionel, he was wounded in Italy on 28 February 1917 but returned to the battalion in May. He later commanded the battalion from 1922 to 1926. (CRO)

Il Comitato Nazionale per la
Medaglia d'onore all'Esercito e al-
l'Armata, istituito in Roma per offrire alla Maestà del Re d'Italia
Vittorio Emanuele III, quale Capo Supremo dell'Esercito e dell'Armata,
una grande Medaglia in oro celebrante la Guerra di redenzione e di
civiltà, ne fece consegna all'Augusto Sovrano il 10 Dicembre 1919.

Il Comitato Nazionale ha inoltre offerta una riproduzione-ricordo
della stessa Medaglia a tutte le Navi ed a tutti i Reggimenti che hanno
partecipato alla Grande Guerra, nonché singolarmente a soldati e marinai
italiani, che maggiormente si sono distinti in fatti d'armi.

Volendo il Comitato Nazionale che l'omaggio sia anche una solenne
testimonianza di plauso per gli Eserciti e le Armate delle forti e valorose
Nazioni alleate, ha deliberato ancora di offrire Loro delle riproduzioni-
ricordo a conferma di sentimenti di sincera fratellanza.

Il presente attestato con una riproduzione in bronzo viene rilasciato a

*The Bucks Battalion, Oxfordshire and
Buckinghamshire Light Infantry*

Roma, li 21 Marzo 1920.

Il Presidente

per la Giunta Esecutiva

Il Presidente

OPPOSITE LEFT: The citation for the medal awarded to the 1/1st Bucks Battalion by the King of Italy, March 1920. (CRO) RIGHT: Lieutenant Colonel L. L. C. Reynolds, who commanded the 1/1st Bucks Battalion from June 1916 until 1922. A High Wycombe doctor, Reynolds briefly commanded 145th Brigade for 15 days in October 1918, one of only three Territorials to do so in 48th Division. (CRO) BELOW: A detachment of 2/1st Bucks Battalion on outpost duty 'waiting for Zepps', as photographed by Captain Ivor Stewart-Liberty at Nevendon near Basildon in Essex, 18 April 1915. (SC) ABOVE LEFT: Geoffry Christie-Miller, who rejoined the Bucks Battalion from the Reserve of Officers in August 1914 and was appointed acting adjutant of the 2/1st. He remained with the battalion until April 1918 when he was appointed to command 2/5th Gloucesters. (CRO) RIGHT: Men of 2/1st Bucks Battalion digging entrenchments at Overstone Park, Northampton, March 1915. Originally billeted in Aylesbury, the 2/1st moved to Northampton on 1 February to join 184th Brigade of 61st (2nd South Midland) Division. (SC) BELOW: H. S. G. Buckmaster (left) and Ivor Stewart-Liberty (right) near Epping, June 1915, the 2/1st Bucks having moved there for a six week camp of instruction. (SC)

ABOVE: The 2/1st Bucks Battalion marching past Lord Kitchener at the review of 61st Division in Hylands Park, 6 August 1915. The battalion always maintained that the favourable impression created did much to persuade the War Office to send 2nd line formations to France. With the exception of the 45th (2nd Wessex) Division sent to India in December 1914, the 61st Division was the first 2nd line Territorial formation to go abroad in May 1916. (BCM) BELOW: A group photograph at the vicarage at The Lee some time before May 1915. Left to right are: 2nd Lt C. P. Phipps, 2/1st Bucks; Col Pownall Phipps, Reserve of Officers; Rev C. Phipps; Capt L. W. Crouch, 1/1st Bucks; Capt G. R. Crouch (married to Joan Phipps), 1/1st Bucks; Capt I. Stewart-Liberty (married to Evelyn Phipps), 2/1st Bucks. In 1916 Charles Phipps and Lionel Crouch were killed and Ivor Stewart-Liberty lost a leg. Another of Rev Phipps' sons died of pneumonia on service in February 1919. (SC)

3/1 Bucks Bn. at Aylesbury, 1915

LEFT: Lt Charles Phipps, 2/1st Bucks Battalion, who was killed, aged 20, in the battalion's first major attack near Laventie on the Somme, 19 July 1916. His brother-in-law, Ivor Stewart-Liberty, was severely wounded in the same attack, only one officer in three attacking companies emerging unscathed. (CRO) RIGHT: The 2/1st Bucks Battalion 'between Chelmsford and Epping' 19 June, 1915. The six weeks camp of instruction at Epping included platoon and company exercises in Epping Forest to test the abilities of the junior officers. (SC) BELOW: The 3/1st Bucks Battalion marching past the LNWR station at the bottom of Aylesbury High Steet, between April and August 1915. Raised by the former CO of the 1st Bucks Rifle Volunteers, Alfred Gilbey, the battalion existed to send drafts to the 1/1st and 2/1st Bucks. (CRO)

89

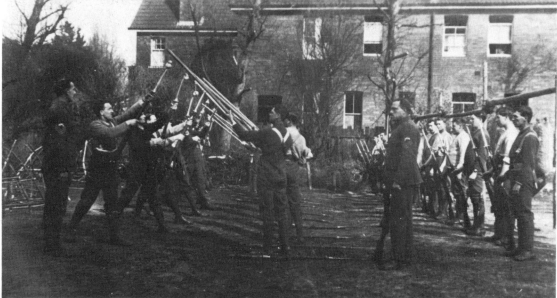

Two photographs of the 3/1st Bucks Battalion in training at Burnham-on-Sea in Somerset, 1916.
Renamed 1st Reserve Bucks Battalion in April 1916, the battalion was then absorbed into the 4th Reserve
Battalion, Oxfordshire and Buckinghamshire Light Infantry. It was successively stationed at Cheltenham,
Catterick and Seaton Delaval, ending the war as part of the Tyne garrison. (CRO)

ABOVE: Men of the Royal Bucks Hussars in the yard of the King's Head, Aylesbury, August 1914. Although the regimental headquarters were at Buckingham, a depôt and recruiting office was opened in Lucas' Pawnbrokers in Walton Street, Aylesbury by Major Coningsby Disraeli. Medicals were held in the King's Head. (CRO) LEFT: B Squadron, 1/1st Royal Bucks Hussars at Whissonsett in Norfolk, autumn of 1914. After a spell under canvas at Churn and Steventon, the 2nd Mounted Brigade, 2nd South Midland Mounted Division undertook anti-invasion duties in East Anglia from November 1914. Pictured centre is Trooper Philip Pitcher of Broughton, Stoke Mandeville who was later wounded at Gallipoli. (MDP) RIGHT: The 2/1st Royal Bucks Hussars in Buckingham, early 1915. Authorised on 14 September 1914, the 2/1st RBH remained in Buckingham until May 1915 before moving to Churn. At Buckingham, billets included the Swan and Castle Hotel, with parades in the Market Square and musketry drill in Hunter Street. (AMOT)

Reg^{tl} Orders by

Col. the Hon. Harry L. W. Lawson J. B. M. P.
Commanding 9st Royal Bucks Hussars.
Thursday 3rd June 1915.

Headquarters,
Yeomanry House,
Part I . Buckingham.

Detail for the day tomorrow.
Orderly Officer   Lieut How
Next for duty   Lieut: Thompson
Reg^{tl} Orderly Serg^t Major S. S. M. Nye
Next for duty   S. L. M. S. Reeves
Reg^{tl} Orderly Serg^t   Serg^t Thompkins.
Line Guard   Thursday L. Cpl. Beale + L. Cpl Long.
Line Guard   Friday   L. Cpl. Jones + L. Cpl. Addison

1.
Parades   Roll call   6. a.m.   (Physical Drill and Stables.)
                                    Water and Feed 7 a.m.
             Parade _ 8.45 a.m. Market Square.
             Riding School 9 - 10 and 11 - 12.
             Men for 9 o'clock ride parade mounted in Paddock.
                                    (Water and Feed 12.30.)
                     Interval 10-30 - 11.
             Rifle Drill, Sword Drill and Physical Drill.
                  Dismiss all parades 12 noon.

2.
Afternoon   Detail as above.
             Parade 2 p.m. Market Square.
             Riding School   2 - 3.
             Men for ride parade mounted in paddock.

OPPOSITE: Orders of the 3/1st Royal Bucks Hussars. Raised in April 1915, the 3/1st remained at Buckingham until sent to Tidworth in July 1915 as part of the 7th Reserve Cavalry Regiment. This, in turn, became absorbed in the 3rd Reserve Cavalry Regiment at Aldershot in 1917. (CRO) ABOVE: Trooper W. G. Pearson, 2/1st Royal Bucks Hussars at Thorndon Park, near Brentwood, 1917. From Churn the 2/1st moved to King's Lynn then to Upminster, Thorndon and Much Hadham before returning to Thorndon in May 1917. Drafts were found for many regiments, Trooper Pearson being drafted to the Gloucestershire Regiment and being taken prisoner in April 1918. (WP)

OPPOSITE ABOVE: Officers of 1/1st Royal Bucks Hussars, 1914. The regiment took part in the attack on Chocolate Hill on 21/22 August suffering 107 casualties. It was withdrawn to Egypt in November 1915. (LP) CENTRE: Traditionally captioned as the 1/1st Royal Bucks Hussars landing at Suvla Bay in August 1915. As that disembarkation took place at night, this seems unlikely, and it probably depicts scenes after the torpedoing of SS *Leasowe Castle* on 26/27 May 1918 while conveying the regiment to France from Egypt. Two members were drowned and all equipment lost, including the 'dizzie'. (LP) BELOW: The 1/1st Royal Bucks Hussars 'at rest' at Mena in Egypt, 1915. The regiment was reunited after Gallipoli as part of the Western Frontier Force operating against Senussi tribesmen on the Libyan frontier, the Senussi being a fanatical sect induced to fight the British by Turkish agents. The campaign continued until October 1916. (NAM) ABOVE: An unidentified photograph of the 1/1st Royal Bucks Hussars 'somewhere in the Middle East'. Following the conclusion of the Senussi campaign, the 6th Mounted Brigade of which the regiment formed part, took part in the defence of the Sinai peninsula against the Turks including the two battles of Gaza in March and April 1917. (CRO) BELOW: The 1/1st Royal Bucks Hussars 'just before moving to outposts' in Palestine, 1917. The 6th Mounted Brigade, now part of the Yeomanry Mounted Division, moved into Palestine in the general advance of General Sir Edmund Allenby's forces of October 1917. (NMR)

ABOVE: The celebrated painting of the charge of the 1/1st Royal Bucks Hussars at El Mughar, 13 November 1917 by J. P. Beadle. At left is the left-handed Major Crocker Bulteel and, at right, is Lieutenant (later Captain) C. H. Perkins who had carried out a reconnaissance under fire prior to the charge. Captain Perkins has described the sensation of the charge as one of being constantly knocked in the face by a pillow from the blast of fire directed at the regiment. (NAM) LEFT: A lesser known version of the action at El Mughar by T. C. Dugdale. Coming up against a Turkish position, the 6th Mounted Brigade, in the words of Major Frederick Lawson, did 'what in its way was one of the greatest things in the war, charging across the open against 3,000 unbroken infantry with guns and machine guns and capturing 1,400 prisoners, two guns and 14 machine guns'. The RBH had 65 casualties including Major the Hon Evelyn de Rothschild who was mortally wounded. (LP) RIGHT: Lt Colonel the Hon F. H. Cripps, 1/1st Royal Bucks Hussars, 1918. With what can only be described as *élan*, Cripps commanded at El Mughar (for which he received the DSO) and subsequently in France where the regiment served from July 1918 in the 101st (Bucks and Berks) Battalion, Machine Gun Corps. (LP)

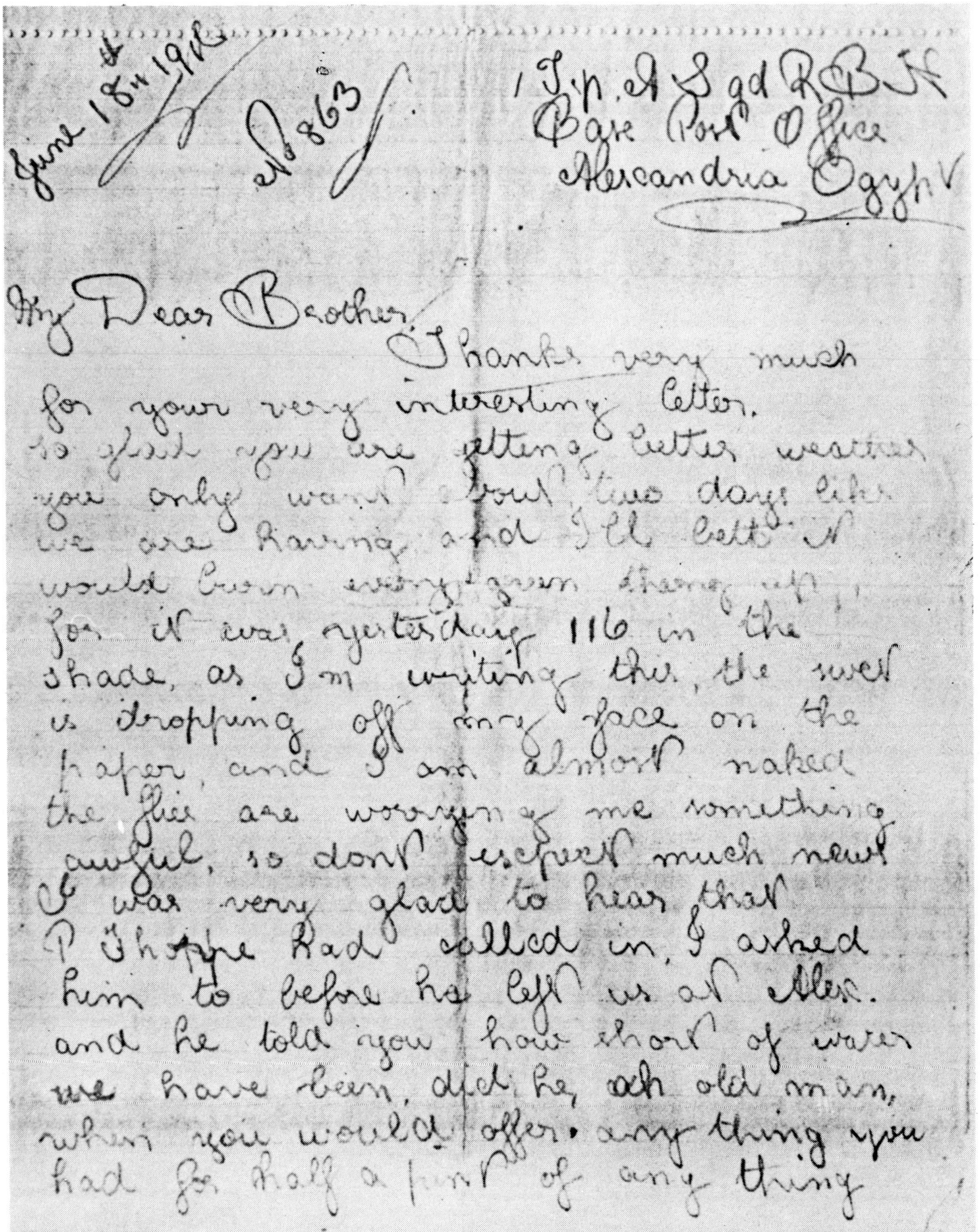

June 18th 1916

No 863

1 T.p.A.Sqd R.B.H.
Base Post Office
Alexandria Egypt

My Dear Brother,

Thanks very much for your very interesting letter. So glad you are getting better weather, you only want about two days like we are having and I'll bett it would burn everygreen thing up, for it was yesterday 116 in the shade, as I'm writing this, the sweat is dropping off my face on the paper, and I am almost naked, the flies are worrying me something awful, so don't expect much news. I was very glad to hear that P Thorpe had called in, I asked him to before he left us at Alex. and he told you how short of water we have been, did he, oh old man, when you would offer any thing you had for half a pint of any thing

Extract from a letter from Trooper W. J. Hilsdon, A Squadron, 1/1st Royal Bucks Hussars from the Base Post Office, Alexandria, 18 June 1916. The letter refers to the heat of Egypt — in Palestine, some relief could occasionally be had by sea bathing in the lull between the end of the Gaza operations and the beginning of Allenby's offensive. (DHT)

Your kind assistance is desired.

G. R

County of Buckingham
Territorial Force Association.

RECRUITING FOR THE REGULAR ARMY AND TERRITORIAL UNITS.

500 MEN ARE REQUIRED

From BUCKINGHAMSHIRE to complete the

8th Battalion of the
Oxfordshire and Buckinghamshire
Regiment.

Standard Height 5ft. 4ins.   Chest 34½in.
Age 19 to 38 years.

Recruits can be enlisted at any Recruiting Centre and sent to the Depôt at Oxford.

RECRUITS also Required, Riding Men, for the

Royal Bucks Hussars
Reserve Regiment,

Apply to their Headquarters at Buckingham, or their Depôt, Walton Street, Aylesbury.

THE

Bucks Reserve Battalion

Require RECRUITS. Apply to the Headquarters, Temple Square, Aylesbury.

GOD SAVE THE KING.

"Bucks Advertiser" Co., Ltd., Aylesbury.

OPPOSITE LEFT: The Recruiting Office in Temple Square, Aylesbury. Officers of the 3/1st Bucks Battalion standing outside indicate a date between April and August 1915. The premises had been taken over by the County Territorial Association in 1909 when the Bucks Battalion headquarters was moved back from Marlow, its location since 1872. (CRO) RIGHT: A handbill which indicates that the County Association was equally concerned to fill the 8th OBLI of the 'New Army' and the 2/1st Bucks Battalion and 2/1st Royal Bucks Hussars. 'No vacancies at present' has been written across the latter's entry. (CRO) BELOW: A recruiting meeting at Marlow in 1914. Although less common after 1915, public meetings remained a staple method of recruiting. A similar format was almost always followed — at Chalfont St Giles in late August 1914, for example, the village band played patriotic tunes, the rector and two other local worthies then made speeches and nearly 40 men were enlisted. (BB) ABOVE: A rather dramatic recruiting poster for the Bucks Battalions from a series of posters issued by the Parliamentary Recruiting Committee. The background was standard with slogans and regimental details (including the cap badge) added as required by local recruiters. (CRO)

TOWN HALL, SLOUGH.

Saturday, 21st November, 1914.

SONGS

To be sung during the Evening.

The Red, White and Blue.

Sung by Mr. OLDS.

Britannia, the pride of the ocean,
  The home of the brave and the free,
The shrine of the sailor's devotion,
  No land can compare unto thee.
Thy mandates make heroes assemble,
  With victory's bright laurels in view,
Thy banners make tyranny tremble
  When borne by the Red, White and Blue.

  When borne by the Red, White and Blue,
  When borne by the Red, White and Blue;
  Thy banners make tyranny tremble,
  When borne by the Red White and Blue.

When war scatter'd wide desolation
  And threaten'd our land to deform,
The ark then of freedom's salvation
  Brittannia rode, safe thro' the storm
With her garlands of vict'ry around her,
  As nobly she bore her brave crew,
With her flag floating bravely before her,
  The flag of the Red, White and Blue.

  CHORUS.

The wine cup of Union bring hither
  And fill it right up to the brim,
May the mem'ry of England ne'er wither
  Nor the star of her glory grow dim.
May France from dear England ne'er sever,
  But each to her colours prove true,
So the Army and Navy for ever
  And three cheers for the Red, White and Blue.

  Three cheers for the Red, White and Blue,
  Three cheers for the Red, White and Blue;
  So the Army and Navy for ever
  And three cheers for the Red, White and Blue.

A song sheet from a recruiting meeting at Slough, 21 November 1914. (CRO)

ABOVE: King George V visiting troops billeted at Great Missenden, 18 November 1914 (SC), and BELOW: Halton Camp, 1914. It was not, of course, just Bucks men who were seen in uniform in the county. Aylesbury, High Wycombe and surrounding villages all had large numbers of troops billeted in 1914. In particular, the 21st Division of 'Kitchener's Army' was concentrated at Halton Park in September 1914, thus beginning the association of Halton with the armed forces. (BB)

COUNTY OF BUCKINGHAM

SPECIAL CONSTABULARY

1914—1919

THIS IS TO CERTIFY that

Mr. *George Eland*

of *Weston Turville*

served in the *Wendover* Company of

The Buckinghamshire Special Constabulary

from *September 5th* , 1914 , to *August 31st* , 1919 , as

Special Constable

and the thanks of the COUNTY are hereby conveyed to him for good
and efficient public service rendered during the GREAT WAR.

Charles G. Wrigley

Captain of the *Wendover* Company.

Otway Mayne , Major,

Chief Constable of Bucks.

Alexander Finlay , Lt.-Col.

Chairman of the Standing Joint Committee
for the County of Buckingham.

Lincolnshire

Lord-Lieutenant of the County of Buckingham, and
Chief Commandant of the Special Constabulary.

COUNTY CONSTABULARY HEADQUARTERS, AYLESBURY,

September 1st , 1919.

OPPOSITE ABOVE: One of the most familiar wartime sights in Aylesbury must have been bodies of troops marching past the LNWR station in the High Street. (BCM) LEFT: A Special Constable's Certificate of Service, 1914-18. The Captain of the Aston Sandford Company of the Bucks Special Constabulary was one who was apprehensive in August 1914 at the prospect of unarmed Specials tackling armed saboteurs. Later the Specials and the Volunteers clashed over which would take first call on a man who happened to be in both in the event of an emergency. (CRO) RIGHT: Private Tommy Smith of Lower Green Farm, Chearsley, 2nd Bucks VTC. Initially no uniform was worn other than an armlet with 'GR' which led to the nicknames of 'George's Relics' and 'Grandpapa's Regiment' among others. (MW/H) ABOVE: The prize winning team from the 4th Battalion, Bucks Volunteer Regiment in 1916. Conventional military titles were not used for commissioned or non-commissioned ranks until after December 1916: hence the Platoon Commander (rather than a Lieutenant) and the Platoon Sergeant. (BBO)

Every Man must to-day honestly face the Question:

Am I a Shirker or am I doing my Share?

In the outward peacefulness of our Country some of us almost forget that German hatred will spare no effort to destroy all that makes our lives worth living.

Every Man must do something to combat this terrible peril.

Let each one ask himself—WHAT CAN I DO?

Every man who possibly can do so has a clear call to enlist in the Regular Army. A thousand extra men in Flanders will bring peace nearer than ten thousand at home.

Many, however, are disqualified by age or health for foreign service, while others are unable to enlist for genuine reasons as, for example, those whose departure from business would bring destitution to numbers of workpeople.

To those who, for good and sufficient reason, cannot join the Regular Army, the Bucks Volunteer Corps appeals.

Those under 38 years of age cannot, under the War Office ruling, be formally enrolled unless they agree in writing to enlist if, in the opinion of the competent Military Authority, they have not a genuine reason for not joining the Regular or Territorial Army.

[P.T.O.

Recruiting handbill for the Gerrards Cross Company of the 4th Battalion, Bucks Volunteer Training Corps — dating from after April 1915, when the battalion was created from within the existing 1st Battalion, in which the Gerrards Cross Company had originally been raised. (CRO)

Indifferent Defences 1919-1939

The Territorial Force was by no means automatically reconstituted after the First World War. Indeed, the Territorials did not fit easily into the post-war military situation; there seemed little likelihood of invasion and part-time volunteers were clearly unsuitable for long-term garrisons in the greatly expanded Empire. The War Office foresaw a Territorial role in medium scale wars which fell short of the need for conscription, but this was opposed by the Treasury. Territorials themselves were wary of undertaking any obligations, without firm guarantees of unit integrity. The difficulty was thus to find some form of obligation acceptable to Territorials, while sufficiently flexible for War Office use overseas.

Negotiations on the terms of reconstruction dragged on from February 1919 until January 1920, before a satisfactory formula was found. Known as the 'Pledge', the compromise sought a Territorial liability for overseas service, against guaranteed integrity of Territorial units. However, the liability was still hedged with legislative requirements, since the force could only be called out by Royal Proclamation after the Army Reserve had been called out (for 'imminent danger or great emergency'), and needed Parliamentary sanction before it could actually go abroad. So the Territorials could not be used by the War Office for the purpose envisaged, since conscription would be introduced for a major war; the impossibility of drafting Territorials where required rendered them unusable in the opening stages of a conflict.

The reconstituted force began recruitment on 1 February 1920, the changed conditions of enlistment legislated for in the Territorial and Reserve Forces Act of 1921. This superseded previous legislation such as the Volunteer Act of 1863 and that of 1901, and also changed the name of the Special Reserve back to Militia, and the Territorials into the Territorial Army. There were other changes, too, for the desire for a more balanced modern army led to proposals to alter the role of the 56 existing yeomanry regiments. Three were to be abolished, the fourteen senior regiments retained as mounted units (these being inexplicably re-armed with swords in 1920), and the remainder were to become mechanised units, signallers or artillery. The Bucks County Association had urged in September 1919 that rural yeomanry regiments be retained rather than any in urban areas, and the Association vigorously protested when the fate of the Royal Bucks Hussars became known in February 1920. Opposition proved fruitless, and in March 1921 the Bucks were combined with the Berkshire Yeomanry in the 99th (Bucks and Berks Yeomanry) Brigade, RFA, two batteries being found by each county. After discussion between Lt Colonel F. H. Cripps and Lt Colonel L. L. C. Reynolds, it was decided to raise 393 (RBY) Battery at Aylesbury, Buckingham and Wing under the command of Major E. P. D. Pauncefort-Duncombe and 394 (RBY) Battery at High Wycombe, Chesham and Taplow under the command of Major E. F. Lawson. The reconstituted Bucks Battalion was located at High Wycombe and Marlow (A Company), Aylesbury and Chesham (B Company), Slough (C Company), and Buckingham and Wolverton (D Company).

In Bucks, as elsewhere, what were to be the first camps of the new Territorial Army in 1921 were threatened with disruption by the miners' lock-out dispute. During the debate on reconstitution, Haldane's decision that Territorials should not be used in aid of the civil power was questioned. The War Office disliked the idea and, during the railway strike of 1919, it was decided to raise a Civic or Citizen Guard though the strike collapsed before this could be implemented. In April 1921 the War Office again declined to embody the Territorials, but on 8 April it was announced that a Defence Force would be raised, reservists being called up simultaneously. By 18 April some 70,000 men had been enrolled, Territorials specifically encouraged to do so and Territorial premises utilised. A Territorial had to resign from the TA, but service in the Defence Force counted towards his Territorial obligation and, if wished, a man could be automatically re-enlisted once the Defence Force was disbanded. A Bucks Battalion was raised and served at Didcot from 13 April to 5 July 1921. It is not clear how many Territorials enlisted, but many officers certainly did so. Geoffry Christie-Miller, for example, served as a Temporary Major although a Lt Colonel on the Territorial Reserve, and the battalion was commanded by Reynolds. Many good Territorials, of course, could hardly give up three months for it and it would appear that many Defence Force personnel were unemployed. As a whole the Defence Force personnel were unemployed. As a whole the Defence Force was not a great success, but the concept was repeated for the General Strike in 1926 in the form of a Civil Constabulary Reserve. Recruiting began on 10 May 1926, but was suspended when the strike collapsed five days later. In Bucks some fourteen serving Territorial officers assisted in raising the CCR and Territorials were again encouraged to enlist. A total of 3,570 Special Constables were also raised, with groups at Wolverton, Slough, Aylesbury and High Wycombe. There was some crowd trouble at Wolverton, but only 28 individuals were brought to Petty Sessions. The idea of the Civil Constabulary Reserve was kept in abeyance until 1939, when it was finally dropped.

Apart from the temporary disruption caused by the creation of such ad hoc bodies, and the dangers posed by associating the Territorials with aid to the civil power, the TA was also badly affected by financial restraint throughout the inter-war years. The War Office tended to regard the TA as that part of the army least relevant to Imperial defence, and the Territorials took the brunt of cuts. A £1 million reduction in the training grant in 1931 led to the cancellation of summer camps the following year. In Bucks a voluntary week's camp was hastily arranged at Marlow, the men attending without pay. As a result, when the military authorities raised the question of the pledge in that year, associations responded with a 'camps for pledge' proposal that the War Office could not accept, since financial decisions were not theirs to make. Once camps were restored in 1933, the War Office again raised the issue of the pledge, and the Council of County Territorial Associations agreed to forego it, provided it did not affect serving Territorials or those who re-enlisted after April 1934. However, not all associations belonged to the Council and, when the War Office gave an assurance to another association that it would honour the pledge, the whole abolition agreement was nullified and the matter dropped once more. Other financial reductions included abolition of the efficiency bounty in 1927, in favour of smaller proficiency grants, while uniform allowances and officers' messing allowances had fallen victim to retrenchment back in 1922. No marriage allowances were granted men under 26 years of age until 1935, and accommodation was not significantly improved until after 1937. The Bucks Association did manage to open a new headquarters in Oxford Road, Aylesbury in 1934, but not without a struggle, since they had previously purchased the George Bodega in the Market Square in 1920, and opened it as a headquarters in March 1922.

Although it was accepted that Territorials could not expect financial reward, the reductions affected recruitment. There were some attractions. The opportunity of two weeks' holiday was a draw, especially at seaside camps such as those held by the Bucks Battalion at Weymouth (1924, 1935), Swanage (1931) and Porthcawl (1937). The use of clubs in Territorial premises was also a major attraction, so much so that the Association rejected a suggestion by Colonel E. F. Lawson in July 1927, to make a recruitment film on the grounds that the money would be better spent on recreational facilities. The new drill hall at Marlow was also opened in 1935, in the belief that the old one hindered recruitment through lack of facilities. Similarly, a survey of recruitment carried out between November 1934 and February 1935 by A. C. Devereux, managing director of High Duty Alloys, concluded that clubs, camps and sport were the major recruiting factors. By 1936 it was felt that camps had lost their attraction, but sport remained important, and there is little doubt that prestige accrued to the Bucks Battalion from its four successive appearances in the final of the TA Association Football Championship, from 1935/6 to 1938/9. Yet, it appears that the majority of recruits for both Bucks Battalion and Yeomanry between the wars were simply brought in by their friends.

In his survey, Devereux had suggested that camps were too long at 15 days, from the viewpoint of the employer. Drills were not a particular problem, being ten for trained infantry and 20 for trained artillerymen, but the second week at camp proved difficult. As early as June 1920 the Bucks Association had sought concessions from local employers. A number had responded well in terms of allowing the second week, including Hazells and Hunt Barnard in Aylesbury, McCorquodales and the LNWR at Wolverton, Wethereds at Marlow and some local authorities, such as the Wolverton and Marlow Town Councils. Others had at least expressed support but not one of 60 High Wycombe employers bothered to reply. In later years other employers were co-operative, such as the Soho Mills at Wooburn, Bucks County Council and Bells' Asbestos at Slough, the Trading Estate opened in 1925 on land previously requisitioned by the Government's Motor Repair Department. In Aylesbury many firms gave prizes for the annual shooting competitions, while Hazells was a model employer in granting not only holiday pay for the full two weeks but a £1 grant towards every married employees' camping expenses: the firm's silver band was virtually duplicated in the Bucks Battalion.

But if some employers were generous, this did not imply that their employees were always well disposed towards the Territorials. In Wolverton the mood had changed considerably with only a platoon, where there had been two full companies prior to 1914. Similarly, Devereux had discovered that most of his employees were indifferent or apathetic to the TA in 1934. In some areas unemployment was a factor in recruitment, particularly around High Wycombe, but this was not significant elsewhere. The Territorials were only at 50% of establishment in 1922 and, with 715 men in total, represented only 0.62% of the male population in 1924. In that year recruiting was especially bad in the north of the county, many men not re-engaging on the expiry of their four years (three years in the case of former Defence Force personnel). The north continued a problem area, officers being particularly short. Although recruiting was generally better in the south, some areas there also had difficulties, Taplow 'drying up' in 1926/7 and the Bucks Battalion's machine gun platoon having to be moved to High Wycombe. Recruiting had picked up considerably by 1938, the Bucks Battalion being at its greatest strength since 1918, but it was still the weakest battalion in its brigade in numbers.

By 1938, the overall situation was improving. Territorials had become eligible for divisional commands in 1922, but the old prejudice of Regular soldiers remained. By 1936 only eight of 50 Territorial brigades had Territorials in command but, under Hore-Belisha as Secretary of State for War, the first Territorial Major-General was appointed to an administrative appointment in October 1937, and the first Territorial divisional commander in the following year. In 1932 the Territorials had taken over major responsibilities for coastal defence, and in 1936 and 1937 two divisions were converted to an anti-aircraft role. This total had risen to five by 1938, with a further three divisions motorised. The Bucks Association was asked to form the 251st AA Battery at Slough in November 1938, other existing TA anti-aircraft units having been called up during the Munich crisis. A Bucks ATS was also established in October 1938, while the recruitment of ARP personnel began in December 1938.

The greatest change in the fortunes of the Territorial Army came in the wake of Hitler's occupation of the remainder of Czechoslovakia in March 1939, Hore-Belisha and Chamberlain making a spur-of-the-moment decision to double the size of the Territorials on 29 March. On one level this persuaded Territorial Assocations to agree to the abolition of the Pledge, although assurances were still sought that Territorials would not be drafted indiscriminately. At another, the increase in establishment from 170,000 to 340,000 set back the preparations being made to modernise the TA, for too few trained officers and men were available. The Bucks Battalion was split, with the Aylesbury, Amersham and Wolverton companies becoming the nucleus for the 1st Battalion, and those at Marlow, Slough and High Wycombe becoming the nucleus of a new 2nd Bucks Battalion by 1 June 1939. By 4 May 1939 the yeomanry had also completed its expansion, the Bucks becoming 99th (RBY) Field Regiment, RA and the Berks Yeomanry becoming the 145th Field Regiment. By this time, too, conscription had been revived, the Military Training Act of 26 May 1939 (following the announcement of 27 April 1939) proposing to call up all those attaining the age of twenty for six months with the colours and 3½ years in the Territorials. In the event, only one group was ever called up of these so-called 'militiamen', as the National Service (Armed Forces) Act introduced conscription for all aged 18 to 41 years in September 1939. A schedule of reserved occupations had been drawn up as early as 1922, to avoid the problems of the previous world war, but it had not been applied to service in the Territorials, with the result that some 12,000 men were immediately lost, the Territorial Army being embodied for the first time on 1 September 1939.

Officers of the Bucks Battalion, OBLI Defence Force at Didcot, May 1921. Described as a 'long hot summer under canvas', little was actually achieved. The chief object of the officers' attention appears to have been the regular disappearance of the mess sergeant to attend races at Epsom, Newbury and Ascot.
(EV)

LEFT: Lt Colonel F. H. Cripps, 1919, remained in command of the Royal Bucks Yeomanry until 1922, and worked in civilian life for Boulton Brothers, being arrested when an Indian bank connected to the firm failed in 1923. He was acquitted of all charges but did not return to military life despite efforts by Lord Cottesloe in 1928 to have him reinstated. (LP) RIGHT: General Sir George Higginson talking to Captain A. D. Burnett-Brown at Marlow, August 1926, on the occasion of his inspection of the Bucks Battalion. Aged 100, Higginson had been one of the few Regular officers to take the old Volunteer Force seriously while GOC, Home District from 1878 to 1885. (BBO) BELOW: Officers' Mess of the Bucks Battalion, Marlow, 1926. Finding officers was a constant problem, Elliott Viney who joined the battalion in 1932 becoming a major at the age of only 25. It also meant considerable sacrifice, Oscar Viney never having a full holiday with his family while commanding between 1930 and 1934. (CRO)

ABOVE: The Bucks Battalion *en route* to Brook camp on the Isle of Wight, 1930, complete with horse transport in the barge towed behind the steamer. (BBO)

OPPOSITE BELOW & ABOVE: Three photographs of the Bucks Battalion that illustrate the way in which the Territorials remained an essential ingredient in local pageantry in the inter-war years. The first two were taken during the visit of the Duke of York to Aylesbury for the opening of the extension to the Royal Bucks Hospital, 2 July 1928 and the third shows the *feu de joie* being fired in Aylesbury Market Square to celebrate the Jubilee of King George V, 6 May 1935. (CRO)

ABOVE: The Adjutant, Capt W. L. Barnard (left) and Lt Colonel Oscar Viney leading the Bucks Battalion from the camp at Swanage, 1931. Seaside camps were usually interspersed with county locations (invariably Marlow) and inland sites such as Chiseldon (1927), Windmill Hill (1933), Marlborough (1934) and Bulford (1938). (EV) BELOW: The 99th (Bucks and Berks Yeomanry) Field Brigade, RFA was horse-drawn until 1926, tractors gradually being introduced after delays in introducing mechanisation and the process not being completed until 1928. The Association secretary, Col F. R. Sedgewick wrote in September 1926 that the yeomanry did not seem to mind 'but I should think the bodies of the Grenvilles will turn in their graves'. (CRO) OPPOSITE ABOVE: 4.5″ Howitzers of 394(RBY) Battery of 99th Field Brigade in the 1930s, 393 Battery being armed with 18 pounders. In February 1937 the yeomanry were described as being engineering men rather than the farmers of old, 394 Battery in particular drawing many recruits from Slough Trading Estate. (WTC) CENTRE: The officers of 99th (Bucks and Berks Yeomanry) Field Brigade, RA at Medmenham Camp, August 1936. Camps were usually alternated between Bucks and Berks, Bucks men invariably shouting 'Rarebits' at the Berks (after the White Horse at Uffington) and the Berks responding with 'Quack-quack'. Seated right front is the right-wing MP for Aylesbury, Captain M. W. Beaumont. BELOW: Men of the Bucks Battalion firing bren guns at the last peacetime camp at Lavant, August 1939. The battalion only received its first bren gun carrier at Lavant and had only one bren gun per company while the anti-tank platoon had no anti-tank weapons. (BBO)

112

ABOVE: Bren Gun Carriers of the 1st Bucks Battalion passing in review before the Duchess of Kent at Newbury, December 1939. Mobilised at Aylesbury, the battalion had moved to Newbury Racecourse in September 1939, remaining there until January 1940. In the leading carrier is 2nd Lieutenant Laurence Viney. (EV) BELOW: Sergeant R. Disbury, 1st Bucks Battalion, bargaining with a local trader at La Neuville, 11 May 1940. After three days of anti-parachute training, the battalion moved into Belgium on 14 May. Withdrawal began three days later, seven positions being dug and abandoned before the battalion reached Hazebrouck. (EV)

From Dunkirk to D-Day 1939-1945

In September 1939 Territorial status was suspended for the duration, by the passage of enabling clauses in the Armed Forces (Conditions of Service) and Military and Air Forces Acts, which removed all anomalies on liability and transfer. Since the preparation of the Territorial Army had been disrupted by the doubling of the force without prior consultation, many units were short of both trained manpower and equipment. The 1st Bucks Battalion, for example, found itself 'fighting the bogey of inexperience', and managed only one battalion, one brigade and one divisional exercise before the 48th Division was despatched to France in January 1940. There was much cross-posting to even out strengths in Territorial units and, once in France, units were interchanged between Regular and Territorial formations. Most Territorial divisions received a regular battalion and, in turn, regular divisions received up to three Territorial battalions. The 1st Bucks Battalion was not affected, but the 99th Field Regiment, having arrived with 48th Division, was transferred to the 2nd Division, to become part of the divisional artillery support, together with 10th and 16th Field Regiments and 13th Anti-tank Regiment.

Thereafter, the Territorials had as much or as little training as the remainder of the army, the 1st Bucks being mostly employed in digging defences and repairing roads in the area of Wahagnies. One draft received in April 1940 had had only six months' training, and there was virtually no practice ammunition available. Judged by such criteria, the subsequent performance of Territorial formations during the German 'Blitzkrieg' of May 1940 was quite remarkable. The 99th Field Regiment suffered heavily in support of 6th Infantry Brigade at St Venant on the La Bassee Canal on 27 May, while the defence of Hazebrouck by the 1st Bucks Battalion between 26 and 28 May 1940 was described in a German broadcast as 'truly worthy of the highest traditions of the British Army'. The battalion had been sent there on 24 May, less A Company, which had become detached some days previously during the withdrawal simply because, as rear battalion of 145th Brigade, they were the easiest to send. Arriving just as GHQ was evacuating the town, the acting commanding officer, Major B. K. Heyworth, a 33-year-old Treasury solicitor from Beaconsfield, was given just one map and no details of the forces available. A defence was organised by the time the Germans appeared in strength at about 1200 hrs on 27 May. The action that followed was acknowledged by the Germans as having delayed their advance for a crucial 48 hours although, in the process, the battalion was all but destroyed; Heyworth was among those killed. Elsewhere Territorials performed equally gallantly, such as the 50th Division at Arras, the 1st Queen Victoria's Rifles at Calais, the 51st Division at St Valery, and the 12th, 23rd and 46th divisions — sent to France only as line of communication and labour troops — south of the Somme. In a report on the battle for France as a whole, the German IV Corps stated that, although less well trained than regulars, British Territorials were the equal of regulars in morale and fighting spirit.

The return of the British Expeditionary Force from France through Dunkirk and other ports unquestionably improved the country's defensive position as to manpower, if not equipment. The prospect of invasion had hardly troubled inter-war planners, since air attack had been consistently considered a more likely eventuality since 1922. After the German advance into the Low Countries and France, and the use of parachutists in particular, opinions were quickly revised, with the expectation that parachutists would be landed prior to seaborne attack. Such seaborne attack was initially envisaged on the east coast, and attention was only shifted to the south coast in September 1940. Thus 99th Field Regiment and both Bucks Battalions found themselves on anti-invasion duties. The 99th Field Regiment was reconstituted after the Dunkirk campaign in the East Riding, with the task of defending Filey, the regiment remaining in the East Riding (apart from exercises) until December 1941, when it moved to Tewkesbury prior to embarkation for India with 2nd Division in March 1942. The 1st Bucks Battalion was reconstituted at Hereford with large drafts received to make up its strength, mostly men from the Somerset Light Infantry, so that by August 1940 some two-thirds were not Bucks men. It was then posted to Devon, and served on anti-invasion duties at Uffculme, Ashburton and Newton Abbot, while providing platoons for fire-watching in Torquay, and for digging defences at Plymouth. The 2nd Bucks Battalion, having remained in Bucks until January 1940, was moved to Hayling Island from Southampton in May 1940, as part of the Portsmouth Garrison Reserve, until it was moved to Northern Ireland in June 1940.

Regulars alone, however, were not judged sufficient for defence against invasion and, in time-honoured fashion, the response to the threat of invasion was also to embrace the raising of auxiliary forces in the form of Local Defence Volunteers. The decision to raise such local forces was taken on 11 May 1940 on the initiative of the C-in-C Home Forces, General Sir Walter Kirke. Kirke was due to make a broadcast, but the new Secretary of State for War in Churchill's coalition government, Anthony Eden, chose to do so himself after the 9 pm news on 14 May 1940. The response to the celebrated broadcast was, of course, immediate, as men aged between 17 and 65 reported to local police stations. At Haddenham, for example, 158 men had enlisted in the first 24 hours, into what was to become A Company of the 4th Bucks Battalion, Home Guard. By 29 May there were 3,584 LDV in Bucks and 18,665 by August 1940, the name Home Guard (coined by Churchill) officially adopted on 23 July 1940. Peak strength was to be the 19,816 of May 1943.

Formal county titles were accorded to the new formations on 3 August, with the county eventually producing thirteen battalions, with headquarters at Aylesbury (1st Battalion), Bletchley (2nd Battalion), Buckingham (3rd Battalion), Marlow (4th Battalion), Beaconsfield (5th Battalion), Taplow (6th Battalion), High Wycombe (7th Battalion), Slough Trading Estate (8th Battalion), Slough Borough (9th Battalion), Langley (10th Battalion), Amersham (11th Battalion), Winslow (12th Battalion) and the Hawker Aircraft Factory at Langley (13th Battalion). The first seven battalions, corresponding to county police divisions, were the first ones formed, with the 8th, 9th and 10th battalions, created from within the 6th Battalion in November 1940; the 11th formed from the 5th Battalion in 1942; the 12th in October 1942; and the 13th from personnel of the 10th Battalion in 1943. The 6th Battalion itself was disbanded in 1942, since most of its men, with some from the 8th, 9th and 10th Battalions, had been transferred to the 101st (Bucks Home Guard) Rocket AA (or 'Z') Battery at Slough in June 1942, and the 71st (Bucks and Berks) HAA Battery, also at Slough, in November 1942. Overall command of the Bucks Home Guard was vested on 17 May 1940 in Colonel P. A. Hall, who had commanded the Bucks Battalion from 1926 to 1930, and had been secretary of the County Territorial Association since 1936. Hall commanded the Bucks Zone (later the

Bucks Sub-Area and, later still, the Bucks Sub-District) until handing over to Colonel G. A. Ledingham, who established his headquarters in Walton House, Aylesbury in February 1942.

There has been a tendency to treat the Home Guard as unique when, in reality, it not only reflected previous auxiliary forces, but strongly resembled the VTC of the First World War in almost all respects. Much has been made, for example, of the conditions of service of the LDV under the Defence Regulations of 17 May 1940, and of the Home Guard under Army Council Instructions of August 1940. The so-called 'Housemaids' Clause', for example, whereby a Home Guard could resign on fourteen days' notice (until November 1941), was no more than a condition written into virtually all volunteer legislation since 1804. Similarly, like the VTC in the First World War, the Home Guard became subject to conscription through the National Service (No 2) Act of November 1941, whereby any male aged between 18 and 51 years could be directed into the force after January 1942, and be compelled to undertake up to 48 hours' duty per month. These 'directed' men were not unlike the 'tribunal' men of 1916-1918, and there are familiar echoes in the complaint of one account of the 6th Battalion that, as a result of their arrival, the 'special spirit dwindled and the atmosphere was less friendly'. Directed personnel were liable to one month's imprisonment or £10 fines for non-attendance, and there were certainly cases brought to court in the 6th Battalion in November 1942, May 1943 and January 1944. There were three cases in the 1st Battalion in September 1943 and, at one petty sessions at Winslow in June 1944, four cases from the 3rd and 12th Battalions were heard at the same sitting. Yet another parallel is the claim of the commander of B Company of the 1st Battalion in September 1943, that concessions granted to agricultural labourers to be absent during harvest, were being abused by non-farm-workers.

More important, like all previous auxiliary forces, there was a steady increase in centralisation and regulation, of which the compulsory direction of men was but one feature. Equipment and weaponry improved gradually with the arrival of denim overalls and Ross rifles and later, of battledress and heavier weapons. In the case of A Company of the 4th Battalion, eight denim suits arrived in May 1940, and battledress in January 1941, although enough was not issued for all recruits until 1944. The company received 200 Ross rifles in August 1940, four Browning automatic rifles in September 1940, two Lewis guns in February 1941, seventeen Thompson sub-machine guns in August 1941, two Northover Projectors in August 1941, Sten guns in July 1942 and a Blacker Bombard in February 1943. In most cases, a great variety of weapons were to be found, C Company of the 1st Battalion mustering 27 .303 rifles, seven 2.2s and 50 shotguns on 28 May 1940, to be distributed among 286 men in an area comprising Ellesborough, Prestwood, The Lee, Stoke Mandeville, Great Missenden and Aston Clinton. In the same month, the 1st Battalion as a whole received just 75 rifles, of which 30 were allocated to the defence of Aylesbury and three to each of 15 surrounding villages. An even older echo was, of course, the issue of the 'egregious pike' as the 4th Battalion history described it, in the autumn of 1941. In the 4th Battalion, and it can be confidently claimed everywhere else, 'it never went beyond the Battalion H.Q. store': in September 1803 Lord Grenville had informed the government that, even though they lacked weapons, no commanding officer of the Bucks Volunteers was willing to accept pikes.

The Home Guard was also reminiscent, for similar reasons, of the VTC in terms of its composition. Detailed enlistment forms were only issued from 1942 and indicated, not surprisingly, that the overwhelming majority of recruits thereafter were manual industrial workers. But, even in 1940, industrial concerns in the county had raised platoons from their employees. In the 1st Battalion there were contingents from Hazells, Hunt Barnard, Northern Dairies, Hills and Partridge and Bifurcated Rivets. The 4th Battalion had one contingent raised for the defence of Jackson's Mill at Marlow while, of course, the 6th

Battalion and its successors were heavily dependent upon the Slough Trading Estate. The 12th Battalion had a contingent from the LMS at Bletchley and the 13th was raised entirely by Hawkers. By contrast, boys of the Stowe OTC were included in the 3rd Battalion, and boys of the Eton OTC in the 6th Battalion. Military experience was varied, rather like the VTC of 1914-18 with, for example, some 23% of the Home Guard at Stoke Mandeville being ex-servicemen: at The Lee one private was General Sir George Barrow. Age also varied quite considerably, although those over 65 had to resign in February 1941, the same month in which officers received commissions, having previously been merely appointed by the Lord Lieutenant. Thus the Home Guard became more recognisably military.

The original perception of the LDV had not actually envisaged much beyond observation and reporting of enemy landings to the local police, hence the epithet of 'Look, Duck and Vanish'. The South Midlands Area advised the Bucks Zone rather helpfully on 18 May 1940 that 'German parachutists are desperate men between the ages of 17 and 50 — fanatics'; further advice was offered by the Air Ministry on 6 June 1940 that they might be disguised as 'British troops, clergymen, nuns, ordinary civilians, etc'. The crucial hours were thought to be from three hours before to three hours after sunrise, the LDV and Home Guard mounting the well known 'dusk to dawn' patrols. At Farnham Royal, the first such patrol went out on 28 May 1940, patrolling possible landing zones on Burnham Grove Estate and to the north of the Trading Estate. In the case of the 1st Battalion, which also raised a mounted section to patrol the Wendover/Kimble/Prestwood area, activity went on until reduced for the winter in October 1940. The greatest danger period of all was judged to be between 8 and 10 September 1940, the codeword 'Cromwell' being issued to eastern and southern counties on the evening of 7 September. As is well known, this was interpreted too literally in some counties and church bells were rung (a proscribed warning device from June 1940 to April 1943) — in Devon the 1st Bucks Battalion was also on alert as was the 99th Field Regiment in Yorkshire. On 9 September a strict order was issued that the bells should only be rung if an individual Home Guard commander personally witnessed the arrival of at least 25 German parachutists. In Bucks, there had actually been an earlier 'Panic Sunday' on 7 July when many roadblocks were hastily erected.

Such paraborne attack was regarded as the precursor of seaborne invasion, and in the Zone Operational Instructions of January 1941, Aylesbury, Buckingham, High Wycombe, Bletchley, Newport Pagnell and Slough were all declared either 'anti-tank islands' or 'centres of resistance' to anticipated armoured attack. Bucks was still as geographically important as in the Civil or Napoleonic Wars, and the main priority was to keep open the 'main route' from Buckingham through Fenny Stratford to Woburn. The likelihood of armoured attack was finally ruled out in May 1942, but parachute attack on airfields (of which Bucks had fifteen), 'vulnerable points' and communications remained a possibility. By November 1943, operational instructions envisaged only armed sabotage but, with the approach of D Day, plans were updated against the possibility of 'suicide raids', with night guards on vulnerable points and inlying battle platoons at nine locations. The number of vulnerable points was quite staggering. Major vulnerable points amounted to over 20, including repeater stations, water and electricity works, Martin-Baker Aircraft at Denham, ICI Paints at Slough and, of course, Chequers, the Headquarters of Bomber Command at High Wycombe and Bletchley Park, where both the Admiralty Operational Intelligence Centre and the Government Code and Cypher School were located. In 1944 there were also 94 minor vulnerable points while, had there been an invasion, 113 factories were listed for immobilisation. The Home Guard was not, however, responsible for all such vulnerable points. Some like Chequers, Bletchley Park and RAF stations such as Halton, Wing and Bomber Command had their own troops, but the Home Guard was responsible for coming to their relief if necessary. Thus F (Walters

Ash Relief Column) Company of 4th Battalion was earmarked to assist Bomber Command, and M Company of the 1st Battalion earmarked to assist Chequers. Each village and town also had its own defence plans, Invasion Committees being established from August 1941. Similar to the Local Emergency Committees of the Great War, they prepared plans to safeguard essential supplies in an invasion. Secrecy hampered their work, and more publicity was accorded to them from April 1942, but most had ceased to function by June 1943.

In undertaking its tasks the Home Guard was subjected to the same kind of ridicule in some quarters as the VTC before. There was, for example, a long and ultimately fruitless correspondence between D Company of the 1st Battalion and Benskins Brewery in 1941, after one landlord was 'heard to say that those present were more like Boy Scouts than Home Guards, or some such phrase of that kind'. There were also clashes with the ARP and the police, some animosity being caused in Great Missenden when a Home Guard cautioned the Chief Warden in September 1941 for leaving his car unlocked, and not immobilised outside the ARP Centre. The platoon commander at Great Missenden also wrote on one occasion in August 1940 that he feared there was 'an undoubted tendency among LDV once they get a little authority on a road to make full use of it', after police and ARP had been stopped near Ballinger from reaching a bomb scene. Nonetheless, the Home Guard fulfilled an important role, not least in their contribution to morale. The 71st Battery at Slough also brought down one flying bomb on 15 June 1944, firing 146 rounds between January and July 1944: in all 27 flying bombs and two long-range rockets were dropped on Bucks between June 1944 and March 1945 and 2001 HE bombs and 5,633 incendiaries between June 1940 and August 1941. Rather like the VTC, the Home Guard also undertook coastal duties, 5 officers and 48 men of the 1st Battalion doing a week's duty at St Lawrence Bay, Essex in August 1944, before being relieved by a similar contingent from the 3rd Battalion. For the most part, however, the usual fare was one of exercises, until the Home Guard was stood down with relatively little reward on 3 December 1944.

One of the most successful series of Home Guard exercises was the BUZZ series, which also involved regular troops, including the 2nd Bucks Battalion, which returned from Northern Ireland in February 1943 and participated in BUZZ II in March while stationed at Great Missenden. It remained there until October 1943 when it moved to Kent, being successively at Dover, Broadstairs and Winchelsea before disbandment in July 1944. As in the case of the dissolution of the 2nd Bucks in 1918, there was some dismay at the decision, especially when it appeared that the 1st Bucks Battalion might be permanently reduced to cadre in August 1944. In the case of the 1st Bucks, the tour in Devon had ended in November 1941 with a move to Lincolnshire, where there was a routine of exercises, lifting root crops and sending drafts to other battalions. In December 1942, however, the battalion was transferred to 54th Division, just before the 48th Division was converted to a permanent training role. The prospect looked no better in the new formation until, in March 1943, the battalion was selected for training as a beach group responsible for landing men, vehicles and stores across the beaches to be used in any future invasion of the continent. From Suffolk and 54th Division, it moved as No 6 Beach Group in 101 Beach Sub-Area, through a series of training locations such as areas of Wales and Scotland, until quartered at Petworth in May 1944 to await D Day on 6 June 1944.

On D Day an advance party of No 6 Beach Group landed on the first tide, with the remainder landing on the second tide on SWORD beach. Casualties were sustained in the landings in the deep water where landing craft lost their way or lowered ramps too soon. Lt Colonel Sale was also wounded a few days later, when trying to pull ammunition from a burning dump, for which he was awarded the George Medal. By 22 June 1944 the battalion had ceased its beach role, and moved inland to defend the locks at Ouistreham, with the

Beach Group formally dissolved on 10 July. It was at this point that the battalion faced administrative extinction, with drafts sent to a number of other regiments. In turn, drafts were received of questionable quality, and the battalion ended up on routine guard duties in Brussels in October 1944. Lt Colonel Boehm managed, however, to persuade the authorities to give the battalion A1 drafts, and in February 1945 it was designated a 'T' or Target Force battalion, designed to seize and hold installations of special interest. In this capacity it worked for both 2nd British Army and 1st Canadian Army and was responsible for seizing the Krupps testing ground at Meppen in April 1945, and Lord Haw Haw's radio transmitter station at Norden. This role continued more or less until December 1945, the battalion passing into suspended animation at Ghent in June 1946, and being formally wound up in August 1946.

The near extinction of both Bucks Battalions was curiously reminiscent of the struggle of the County Association to keep its formations in being between 1914 and 1918. Indeed, in 1941, Lord Cottesloe as Lord Lieutenant had to conduct a battle to retain the distinctive badge and title of the two battalions. Once more, too, a world war had ended with the immediate prospects for the future of the Territorial Army distinctly gloomy with the lack of a perceived need for the civilian soldier.

Men of the 1st Bucks Battalion as prisoners of war, 1942. The Germans broke through the outlying companies around 2030 hrs on 27 May 1940 and headquarters were completely cut off, Major Elliott Viney and a large party being surrounded by 1800 hours on 28 May. In all, 10 officers and 200 other ranks escaped while the battalion's band instruments, buried at Wahagnies, were recovered in 1944. (RGD)

ABOVE: Men of D (Wendover) Company, 1st Bucks Battalion, Home Guard at Wendover, 1940. The early date is betrayed by the lack of rifles, which have been apparently strategically distributed for effect. The company was offered a double-barrelled elephant gun, Holland and Holland subsequently finding 23 500-bore cartridges, which it offered to sell at 21s plus 2s carriage. (CRO). BELOW: The Chearsley Platoon of D Company, 3rd Bucks Battalion, Home Guard, in front of The Forge at Chearsley, 1940/41. In the back row (second left) is the Rev Elliot Wigg, the church hut being the headquarters while the back of an old van of grocer 'Jimmers' Slater (front second left) was used as an outpost on the hill behind the village. (EG/H)

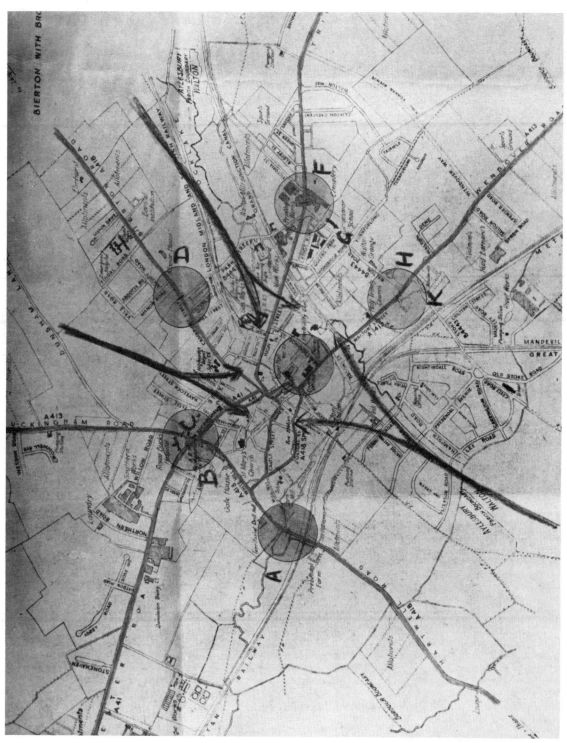

A map attached to the Aylesbury Town Defence Scheme, 7 November 1941. It illustrates the roadblocks, the 'keep' in the area of the County Offices and the location of the 'reserve' in the Drill Hall to be defended, in all, by 592 men. The plan for this 'anti-tank island' was revised in March 1942 and again in 1944. (CRO)

122

ABOVE: The Great Missenden Platoon of C Company, 1st Bucks Battalion, Home Guard, photographed after winning a drill competition at Wendover, 13 September 1942. Commanded by Captain D. D. Goldingham of the National Employers Mutual and General Insurance Company, over 40 per cent were reported in October 1940 as employees of Goldingham's company and another insurance firm, British Oak. (GS) BELOW: The Aylesbury Post Office Section of 10th Berkshire Battalion, Home Guard. Formed in 1941, the section comprised postmen, postal engineers, telephonists and head office staff. Although independent, the section came under command of the 1st Bucks Battalion, Home Guard for the purposes of the defence of Aylesbury. (JS/DR)

ABOVE: The 2003rd (Bucks) Home Guard Mechanised Transport Company at its final stand down parade at High Wycombe, 3 December 1944. Formed in 1943, the company was one of three specialised Home Guard formations in Bucks, the others the 71st and 101st Batteries, both at Slough. (MW/H)
BELOW: Captioned as the 2nd Bucks Battalion on exercise between May and July 1941 although it is conceivable that the official series from which it is taken may actually be of the 1st Battalion. At the time the 2nd were in Northern Ireland, having been put on alert for service in a 'tropical country' only to serve at Ballymena, Ballycastle, Limavady, Enniskillen and Castledown between June 1940 and February 1943.
(IWM)

ABOVE: Present and past officers of the Bucks Battalions photographed when the Duchess of Kent visited the 2nd Bucks Battalion at Great Missenden, 15 May 1943. Included in the back row are Colonel L. L. C. Reynolds (second left); Colonel P. A. Hall (fifth left); and Colonel Oscar Viney (second right). In the front row are Colonel A. D. Burnett-Brown (second left); Colonel Lord Cottesloe (third left) and Colonel G. R. Crouch (first right). (EV) BELOW: Two photographs during the visit of the Duchess of Kent to the 2nd Bucks Battalion, 15 May 1943. The Duchess had unexpectedly been appointed Honorary Colonel of the Bucks Battalion in 1937 when the 3rd Lord Cottesloe was already Honorary Colonel, having commanded the battalion as T. F. Fremantle from 1906 to 1911. The Duchess visited the 1st Bucks Battalion at Newton Abbot in August 1941 and the 2nd on this occasion, having been made its Honorary Colonel, again with Lord Cottesloe, in July 1940. (BBO)

ABOVE: A sadly unidentified photograph of men of the 1st Bucks Battalion which may date from the tour in Brussels between October 1944 and February 1945 before becoming a Target Force battalion. (BBO) BELOW: The Firs at Whitchurch showing the workshops used by M.D. 1 ('Winston Churchill's Toyshop'), who used the premises from 1940 to 1946, producing such weapons as the Sticky Bomb and the Piat. Bucks had many such establishments including the Research and Experiment Branch of the Home Office at Princes Risborough, the SOE Signal Schools at Fawley Court and Grendon Hall and the Home Guard Training Centre at Hedgerley Park.

ABOVE: Lt Colonel J. P. Whiteley MP, with warrant officers and NCOs of 99th Field Regiment at Ahmadnegar, India, 1942. Originally destined for Madagascar, the regiment and 2nd Division arrived in India in March 1942, undergoing training in the Deccan, at Poona and north of Bombay before some personnel were committed to the Arakan in support of 6th Infantry Brigade. Whiteley was later killed in the same plane crash as the Polish General Sikorski on 4 July 1943. (WTC) BELOW: Kohima, 1944. After the Arakan campaign, 99th Field Regiment was reunited and underwent jungle training at Belgaum before moving in support of 6th Infantry Brigade to the defence of Kohima, a major Japanese offensive having begun against Kohima and Imphal in March 1944. 2nd Division relieved Kohima on 18/20 April 1944, 6th Infantry Brigade undertaking a major offensive on 4/7 May. By 6/7 May the Japanese were pulling back after a 64 day battle. (WTC)

128

OPPOSITE ABOVE: Kohima 1944. (WTC) BELOW & ABOVE: Three photographs of 99th Field Regiment's 393 Battery with its 3.7″ howitzers 'on the road to Imphal', June 1944. Having successfully pushed back the Japanese from Kohima, 2nd Division pushed forward to relieve Imphal, the link-up being made on 22 June 1944. The Kohima/Imphal battles were the turning point in the Burma campaign which broke the Japanese XV Army. (WTC)

393 Battery of 99th Field Regiment crossing the Irrawaddy, February 1945. Slim's 14th Army was charged with 'the recapture of all Burma at the earliest date' after the Japanese defeats at Kohima and Imphal. The advance began in December 1944 with 2nd Division crossing the Irrawaddy west of Mandalay. After the town's fall in March 1945, 2nd Division's part in the final offensive was virtually completed, 99th Field Regiment returning to Calcutta in May 1945. (WTC)

Swansong 1945-1985

The post-war story of the military units of Bucks is one of constant change and amalgamation, the Territorial Army being regarded after the Second World War as inappropriate in a missile age. In the process, all real links with past Bucks units were extinguished although, in recent years, the Territorials have once more been restored to a greater role in Britain's defence.

The TA was reformed in March 1947, the county units becoming the 299th (RBY) Field Regiment, RA, replacing the 99th Field Regiment, and the 645th Light AA Regiment replacing the Bucks Battalion. The pre-war 251st AA Battery at Slough was no longer a responsibility of the County Association, but two new units were raised — the 162nd Independent Infantry Brigade Ordnance Field Park, RAOC at Newport Pagnell, and the 56th Medium Workshop, REME at Slough. A WRAC unit was subsequently raised at Slough in 1952. Within 299 Field Regiment, batteries were allocated to Aylesbury, Taplow/Marlow and Buckingham/Bletchley with batteries of the 645 LAA Regiment at Slough, Aylesbury and High Wycombe/Wooburn/Chesham. A major recruiting drive was launched in October 1948 and, by March 1949, the Territorials in Bucks stood at 48 officers and 214 other ranks.

Further change was already under way. In view of the army's desperate need for manpower, to meet both occupation commitments and the growing threat of insurgency in colonial and dependent territories, conscription was retained in the form of national service. It was intended, under the National Service Act of 1947, that national servicemen would serve 18 months with the colours and four years in the TA, but this was changed in 1950 to two years with the colours and 3½ years in the TA. In effect the TA was deprived of the 17-20 age group while national servicemen were only liable to 60 days' training in their 3½ years, including 15 days' camp annually. The true volunteers were liable to 60 hours a year in addition to annual camp, with a bounty offered for an additional 60 hours' training. The problem was that post-war conditions were different from those of the inter-war years, since employment was fuller, and most families could afford a summer holiday. As a result the TA became dependent upon the national servicemen to keep up strength, with over 60% national servicemen by 1960. Of course, national service ended in that year, with the last conscripts due to leave the army in 1963, and the TA by 1966. In any case, manpower was less in demand as technology improved, and after 1955, only two of the TA's ten divisions were actually earmarked as reinforcements for NATO, in defence of western Europe. One rather curious anomaly was the revival of the Home Guard in April 1951, with seven battalions raised in Bucks at Aylesbury, Newport Pagnell, Winslow, High Wycombe, Chesham and Slough (2), but they were only ever raised to cadre strength, and were disbanded in August 1957: the Home Guard Act of 1951 remains on the statute book.

The lowest point for the TA, however, was to come with the gradual evolution of the Labour government's plans between 1965 and 1968. Civil Defence was placed on a care-and-maintenance basis, and even County Associations only just survived extinction. The TA itself became the Territorial and Army Volunteer Reserve in four categories: TAVR I consisted of the former TA Emergency Reserve or 'Ever Readies', formed in April 1962, and other specialists; TAVR II of those units with a NATO role; TAVR III of the bulk of the former TA with only a home defence role;and TAVR IV of miscellaneous units such as OTCs. In November 1968 the first three categories were merged, while the consequent amalgamations as a whole substituted regional affiliations for county loyalties. Not surprisingly, numbers fell rapidly from 116,500 in December 1964 to 54,800 by March 1968.

For the Bucks TA the changes came on top of many already absorbed since 1947. The 299 Field Regiment had absorbed the Oxfordshire Yeomanry in 1950 to become 299 (Bucks and Oxf Yeomanry) Field Regiment, RA, the Bucks losing a battle to retain the Royal title but, in 1952, this was restored with the name changed to 299 (RBY & QOOH) Field Regiment, RA (TA) with two batteries in the county. In 1956 the Berkshire Yeomanry was similarly absorbed in what became 299 (RBY, BY & QOOH) Field Regiment, RA (TA) with only one battery in Bucks distributed between Aylesbury, Taplow and Marlow. The title was changed yet again in 1961 to 299 (RBY, QOOH & Berkshire) Field Regiment, RA (TA) with the epithet 'Field' being subsequently omitted from October 1961 to March 1964, when it was restored. The Bucks Battalion's descendent unit was also absorbed, 645 LAA becoming 431st LAA Regiment in 1955 and, in turn, this was absorbed by 299 Field Regiment in May 1961, at which time the unit had contingents at High Wycombe and Aylesbury/Chesham. The 162 IIB Ordnance Field Park, having spawned 57th Medium Workshop at Wolverton in 1951, became 54th Infantry Division Ordnance Field Park in 1956, while 57th Medium Workshop became 121st Transport Column Workshop, REME in the same year. The 56th Medium Workshop, REME likewise became translated into 50th Medium Workshop in 1960 and was transferred to Aldershot. 54th Infantry Division Ordnance Field Park also changed again in 1960, when it became No 1 Store Company, RAOC.

Under Labour plans for the TAVR, just two troops of 245 Squadron, Royal Corps of Transport and REME in TAVR II were to be raised in Bucks, with 299 Field Regiment replaced in TAVR III by a cadre formation to be known as The Buckinghamshire Regiment, RA (T) while the Bucks County Territorial Association, which had had a joint secretary with Oxfordshire since 1964, became absorbed in the Eastern Wessex Association. The final parades of the Bucks TA units took place in February and March 1966, with the 299 Field Regiment formally ending its existence on 31 March 1967. Its last commanding officer, Lt Colonel L. J. Verney became first commanding officer of the Buckinghamshire Regiment, but this existed only on paper, and was absorbed by the 2nd Wessex Regiment in 1971. At the time of final disbandment, Bucks units totalled 31 officers and 305 other ranks in March 1967, the greatest post-war strength being the 98 officers and 1,660 other ranks of 1954/5.

When disbanded in 1961, the 431st LAA Regiment had theoretically handed the 'traditions' of the Bucks Battalion to the company of the 4th Battalion, Oxfordshire and Buckinghamshire Light Infantry, raised at High Wycombe in 1950. This subsequently extended its recruitment to Slough and Newport Pagnell and remained after the TAVR changes as part of 4th (Volunteer) Battalion of the Royal Green Jackets (the OBLI having become The Green Jackets in 1958 and the RGJ in 1966). It is not, however, a true representative of those auxiliary forces that had existed in the county until swept away in 1967. Nevertheless, the Territorials have survived, and the term 'Territorial Army' was itself restored in April 1982. The modern TA, which has a total strength of some 72,800 men, is now an integral part of the army, in the sense that it comprises 28% of the British army on alert in an emergency. There are also plans for expansion, with a 5th Volunteer Battalion of the Royal Green Jackets to be established in 1986 with companies in Bucks. It is rumoured that the title of the new battalion may revive that of the Oxfordshire and Buckinghamshire Light Infantry, or even that of the Buckinghamshire Regiment. It will not be the same, but it does provide at least some link with centuries of past service by the amateur soldiers of Buckinghamshire.

ABOVE: Yeomanry House, Buckingham, LEFT: before, and RIGHT: after restoration by the University of Buckingham. (UB) BELOW: An eccentric collection of uniforms in the Jubilee celebrations of the TA in Aylesbury in 1958. (CRO)

ABOVE: Gentlemen Cadets of the RMC at Marlow, 1810. In May 1799, what was eventually to become the Staff College, was established in the Antelope Inn at High Wycombe, remaining there until moved to Farnham in 1813. The Junior Division, soon to become the Royal Military College, was established in Remnantz at Marlow in May 1802 until moved to Sandhurst in 1812. Remnantz was later owned by the Wethered family, who had such strong links to the Volunteers and Territorials in Bucks. (AMOT)
BELOW: Staff Officers, attending manoeuvres, on Pitchcott Hill in 1907. One 'army' was stationed at Addington Park and the other at Aylesbury in September 1907, much of the 'action' taking place in the vicinity of Whitchurch, Oving, Pitchcott and North Marston. Similar manoeuvres were held further north in the county in 1913.

The Regular Units

Bucks has had relatively little contact with the Regular army, its military traditions resting primarily in the hands of its civilian soldiers. There have, of course, been many occasions on which regular troops have passed through the county, as in October 1688, when Irish troops passing through East Claydon 'quarrelled amongst themselves about going over a stile in Newfield', with the result that one ended with a broken skull. Parish registers also record the frequent passage of troops. At Aylesbury, for example, an officer was buried in 1707, a drowned solider in 1709, a 'blackamore' musician of Lord Peterborough's regiment in 1713 and three men of Colonel Wade's regiment between 1726 and 1728. Indeed, in the early 18th century, quarter sessions records are also full of references to cases brought to court for refusal to convey troops' baggage. Similarly, it was quite frequent for cavalry regiments to be seen moving through the county in the mid-19th century, the 15th Lancers passing through *en route* to Manchester from Hounslow in June 1851, and the 18th Hussars *en route* from York to Chichester in July 1869. There were also encampments in Bucks during wartime, as at Datchet in 1740, Amersham in 1757 and at High Wycombe in 1800.

In terms of a more permanent link, a number of regular regiments have had some connection with Bucks. The first was the 13th Foot (later the Somerset Light Infantry) raised in June 1685 with headquarters at Buckingham and Aylesbury, until moved to Hounslow in August 1685. The regiment briefly returned to quarters in the county in May and June 1688 but had no links thereafter. Similarly, the 16th Foot, (later the Beds and Herts Regiment), was quartered in Stony Stratford after being raised in Middlesex in October 1685. It left the county in April 1689, but was given the title of the Buckinghamshire Regiment in August 1782, when a county affiliation scheme was instituted. The regiment was allocated High Wycombe as a recruiting location, but the scheme did not survive beyond 1784, and the regiment did not appear in the county again, swopping titles with the 14th Foot in May 1809.

The 85th Foot (later the King's Shropshire Light Infantry) was raised in the county between October 1793 and February 1794 by the 1st Marquis of Buckingham, on behalf of his wife's half-brother's illegitimate son, Sir George Nugent. In all, 520 men were raised, but the regiment was then despatched to Ireland almost immediately, despite assurances by the military authorities that it would not be sent abroad. Recruiting parties were sent back to Buckingham in 1798, and a depôt established there when the regiment returned to England from the West Indies in July 1808, before the regiment again departed the county in September 1808. The Marquis of Buckingham had written in August 1806 that there was no real link remaining with either the 16th Foot, not seen since 1782, or the 85th, which could no longer find recruits after the broken promises of 1794. Thus the 85th, though remaining the 'Bucks Volunteers' until 1827, had little connection with Bucks after 1808.

Buckingham's preference for a regular regiment linked to the county had fallen in 1806 on the 14th Foot. Bucks supplied manpower from the Royal Bucks Kings Own Militia to a number of regiments, such as the 338 men sent to the 4th Foot in 1799, but increasingly they went to the 14th (later the West Yorkshire Regiment). A crucial factor in the growing link was the interest of the Adjutant General, Sir Harry Calvert, who became Colonel of the 14th in February 1806. Calvert was related to the Verneys of Claydon House, his son inheriting the estate in 1827 and changing his name to Verney, and it was Calvert who was instrumental in the 16th and 14th Foot swopping county affiliations in 1809, so that the 14th now became the Buckinghamshire Regiment. The 2/14th received a large draft from the RBKOM in January 1809, when it reorganised at Aylesbury and Buckingham after the evacuation from Corunna; NCOs from the 14th drilled the Bucks Local Militia and a depôt company was established at Buckingham in 1810. When a 3rd battalion was raised at Weedon Barracks in Northants in 1813, it consisted 'principally of Buckinghamshire lads fresh from the plough' and was nicknamed both the 'Bucks' and, from the 'un-buckish' appearance, the 'Peasants'. The battalion was due to be disbanded in March 1815, but was hastily sent to Belgium when Napoleon returned from Elba, and it suffered 28 casualties at Waterloo while in reserve with the 4th Division, mostly from artillery fire.

The 14th remained the county regiment until, under the localisation scheme, it was linked with Yorkshire, becoming in 1881 under territorialisation the West Yorkshire Regiment. At the same time, Bucks fell within the jurisdiction of the 43rd and 52nd Foot, linked as the Oxfordshire Light Infantry. As already indicated, both the RBKOM and the Bucks Rifle Volunteers resisted the change of title and uniform, and attempts were made in 1900, 1914 and 1919 to establish a Buckinghamshire regular regiment. These all came to nothing, but the regiment's title was changed to Oxfordshire and Buckinghamshire Light Infantry in 1908

World War I tank enters Kingsbury Square as a memorial. Subsequently removed, it blew up — with petrol left in its tank from its last journey. (RM)

136

ABOVE: Men of the Oxfordshire and Buckinghamshire Light Infantry in Farnham Royal, 2 October 1913. The 1913 manoeuvres were principally held around Wolverton and Stony Stratford where damage was done to crops to the anguish of many local farmers. (AMOT) BELOW: Unveiling the Buckingham War Memorial, 20 May 1920. (DR)

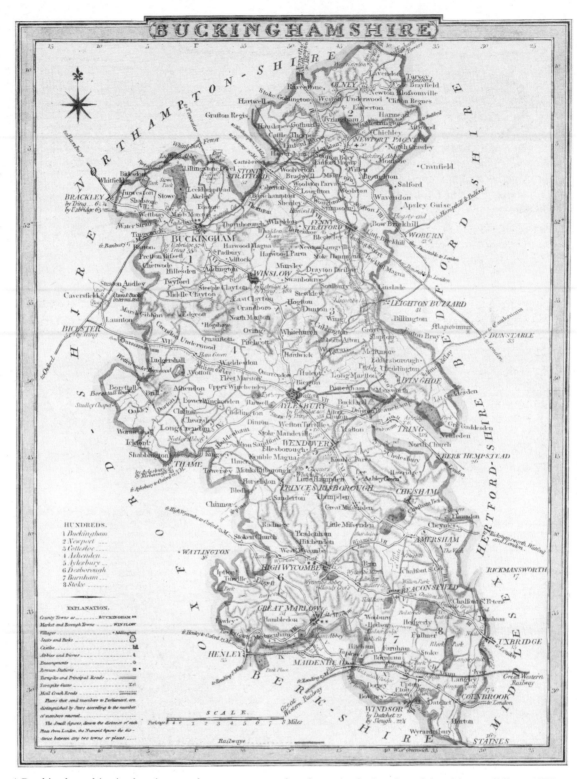

Buckinghamshire in the nineteenth century — much as it was in the heyday of the citizen solidiers. (CB)

Select Bibliography

Bucks Units

L. W. Crouch, *Duty and Service: Letters from the Front* (1917)

P. A. Hall, *A Short History of the Units Administered by the Bucks Territorial and Auxiliary Forces Association* (1950)

L. W. Kentish, *Bux 4: Records and Reminiscences of the 4th Bucks Battalion, Home Guard* (1945)

S. L. Miller, *Old Buck: A Memento for E Company, 7th Bucks Battalion, Home Guard* (1945)

J. C. Swann, *The 2nd Bucks Battalion* (1920)

J. C. Swann, *The Citizen Soldiers of Buckinghamshire, 1795-1926* (1930)

P. L. Wright, *The 1st Bucks Battalion, 1914-1919* (1920)

> *Four Chevrons: The Story of A Company, 4th Bucks Battalion, Home Guard, 1940-1944* (1945)
> *The Oxfordshire and Buckinghamshire Light Infantry War Chronicle* 1914-1918 (4 volumes) and 1939-1945 (4 volumes)

General

I. F. W. Beckett, *Riflemen Form: A Study of the Rifle Volunteer Movement, 1859-1908* (1982)

I. F. W. Beckett and Keith Simpson, *A Nation in Arms: A Social Study of the British Army in the First World War* (1985)

L. Boynton, *The Elizabethan Militia* (1967)

C. Emsley, *British Society and the French Wars* (1979)

Sir J. Fortescue, *The County Lieutenancies and the Army* (1909)

N. Longmate, *The Real Dad's Army* (1974)

P. J. R. Mileham, *The Yeomanry: An Illustrated History* (1985)

C. S. Montefiore, *A History of the Volunteer Force* (1908)

J. D. Sainsbury, *Hertfordshire's Soldiers from 1757* (1969)

J. R. Western, *The English Militia in the Eighteenth Century* (1965)

Key to Caption Credits

NOTE: References —
British Library (BRL): Royal 7 CXVI f 260v (page 12); Stowe Mss 801 f 17 (page 24); Stowe Mss 488 (page 24). Bodleian Library (BL): Ms Top Bucks b6 (page 20). Public Record Office (PRO): E101/67/15(2) (page 21).

AMOT	Army Museums Ogily Trust	LP	Lord Parmoor
BB	Barracuda Books	WP	W. G. Pearson Esq
SB	Mrs S. Bernard	MDP	Mrs D. Pitcher
CB	Clive Birch	PRO	Public Record Office
BL	Bodleian Library	DR	D. Rayner
BRL	British Library	RR/H	R. Roper Esq via T. Hooton Esq
BBO	Bucks Battalion Old Comrades Association	NMR	N. M. Rothschild Archives
BCM	Bucks County Museum	MS	Margaret Sale
CRO	Bucks County Record Office	PS	Mrs P. Stevens
WTC	W. T. Chenery Esq	GS	Major G. M. I. Stroud
SC	Mrs S. Cowdy	JS/DR	J. Suggers Esq and D. Robinson Esq
RGD	R. G. Davies Esq	DHT	Mrs D. H. Tebbutt
EG/H	E. Godfrey Esq via T. Hooton Esq	BMT	Mrs B. M. Turner
IWM	Imperial War Museum	EV	Major E. Viney
RM	Ralph May	PW	Mrs P. Waters
NAM	National Army Museum	UB	University of Buckingham
DP	Mrs D. Page		

141

Subscribers

Presentation Copies

1 The Hon John Fremantle
HM Lord Lieutenant for Buckinghamshire
2 Royal Bucks Hussars Association
3 Bucks Battalion Old Comrades Association
4 Buckinghamshire County Council
5 Buckinghamshire County Library
6 Buckinghamshire Record Office
7 Buckinghamshire County Museum
8 East Wessex Territorial Association
9 Buckinghamshire Military Museum Trust
10 Dr John Clarke

11 Dr Ian Beckett
12 Clive & Carolyn Birch
13 Maj Gen Derek
    Braggins FCIT
    FBIM
14 Maj Gen Peter Blunt
    CB MBE GM FCIT
15 Brig Compton Boyd
16 Barry Mayo
17 Nick Chorlton
18 Alec John Brown
19 Edward Brian Edgar
    Gibson
20 G.A.E. Laming
21 Buckinghamshire
    County Museum
22 Mr & Mrs D.R. Peake
23 R.W. Barnes
24 L.J. Verney
25 Andrew Evans
26 Rev Arthur Taylor
27 Cllr D.A.B. Green
28 George Lamb
29 R.J. Collis
30 Paul M. Lewis
31 David Dee
32 Harry Baker
33 Mrs S.E. Mawby
34 A.H. Woolford
35 Betty M. Turner
36 F.G. Parrott
37 Miss M. Sale
38 J.W. Robins
39 Victoria & Albert
    Museum
40 London Guildhall
    Library
41 Frank Cregan
42 C.T. Wood
43 B.M. Pratt
44 Bob Goodall

45 A.L. Rowley
46 Ted Hooton
47 Ivy Irene Stonell
48 K.M.D. Dunbar
49 A.J. Stonell
50 Dorothy G. Blackman
51 Donald G. Skinner
52 Wellesbourne School
    Resource Centre
53 Colin le Messurier
54 Lt Col E.G.Heath
55 Capt O.R. Warner
56 Thomas R. Whitley
57 C.O. Pilgrim
58 Military Archive &
59 Research Services
60 A.B. Mansfield
61 John Robert Williams
62 C.L. Wilson
63 J.G. Goldsmith
64 National Army
    Museum
65 B. Mollo
66 Richard Sampson
67 Christopher T. Miller
68 David John Melia
69 Bill Grayer
70 Robert Spencer
    Bernard
71 Edward Sammes
72 John J. Morrissey
73 A.F. Bagley
74
77 John Fremantle
78 Buckinghamshire
117 County Library
118 A.J.E. Lloyd
119 Malcolm Sloman
120 E. Legg
121 Antelmi Cosimo
122 Mrs Susan Cowdy

123 Anthony Wethered
124 John H. Ellis
125 Ian W.L. Tindall
126 Joan Brousson
127 Michael T. Roper
128 G.S. Plumridge
129
130 Major S. C. Chapman
131 Kenneth J. Woolley
132 R.F. Copcutt
133 Rt Rev M.A. Mann
134 Lt Col J.O. Jones
    OBE TD DL
135 Michael Rice
136 Mrs J.D. Brousson
137 Michael Kelly
138 A.A. Johnston
139 Anthony Francis
    Skelsey
140 John G. Bailey
141 John Robert Williams
142 Laurence V. Archer
143 Philip J.
    Haythornthwaite
144 F.J.R. Spencer
145 David Drewett
146 Stephen Dance
147 M.S. Marjoram
148 David George
    Matthews
149 Lord Burnham
150 K.B. Hook
151 Barry Boon
152 Clifford Walters
153 Gary Gibbs
154 Malcolm Sloman
155 Lt Col R.J. Wyatt
    MBE TD
156 Gordon Hildreth
157 George Davess
158 Rev Richard Ashton

159 Frederick John Wortley
160 Geoff Mills
161 Robert Kenneth Shepherd
162 Alan W. Collin
163 E.L.F. Barrett
164 B.M. Goodman
165 J. Barry Boon
166 Mrs Yvonne Richardson
167 Ernest Charles Cooper
168 John F. Dennis
169 B. K. Arbery
170 R. A. Westlake
171 J. W. Hunt
172 BA ALA FRSA
173 Buckinghamshire Record Office
174 Miss T.E. Vernon
175 A.G. Curtis
176 Robert J. Ayres
177 Desmond Keen
178 Kenneth W.S. Goodson
179 J.G. Woodroff
180 The Hon David McAlpine
181 Buckinghamshire Archaeological Society
182 C.B. Sandham
183 Jim W. Isaacs
184 W.H. Everett & Son Ltd
185 Elliott Viney
186 Lt Col J.D. Sainsbury TD
187 G. Archer Parfitt
188 Malcolm McGregor
189 Bob Hatch
190 R. Matthews

191 W.A. Townsend
192 R.J. Smith
193 Kenneth C. Pollard
194 L.H.C. Phipps MM
195
196 Ramon Wyre
197 S.J. Kretschmer
198 K.W. Bateman
199 D.H. Morris
200 Major T.L. Craze
201 R.C. Brimmer
202 Oxf & Bucks Lt Inf OCA
203 Edward H. Bailey
204 Richard Ives
205 Michael George Holland
206 Frank E. Atter
207 Margaret M. Jones
208 L. Bunker
209 Mrs M.J. Lacey
210 Lt Col S.W. Orton TD LLB
211 W. West
212 C.W. Kent
213 J.D. Shellabear
214 R.G. Holmes
215 Keith Jeffrey
216 R.A. Beckett
217 Peter T. Scott
218 R.I.L. Rose
219 G.T. Flint-Shipman
220 Duncan Anderson
221 H.F.A. Strachan
222 Capt M.S. Cheetham
223 A. Leggett
224 K.I. Hood
225 David D.A. Linaker
226 Mrs Spencer Bernard
227 Edward Sewell
228 David J. Barnes
229 Lt Col T.B. Wright ALC

230 Miss Thelma E. Vernon
231 Evelyn de Rothschild
232 Lesley Wynne-Davies
233 Dr R.G. Davies
234 Roger Parker-Jervis
235 A.F. Bowden
236 Lt Col R.J. Wyatt MBE TD
237 R.G. Eaton
238 Roland John Jeffrey
239 Peter Brown
240 Sir Ralph Verney KBE
241 Rodney Corner
242 Andrew Corner
243 David Jefferson
244 László L. Gróf
245 Richard O'Shea
246 Sir Francis Dashwood Bt
247 D.L. Scrimshaw
248 Robert J. Smith
249 M.G. Prevezer
250 Rev Richard Ashton
251 Mrs Constance Marshall
252 The Chalfont County Secondary School
253 J.B. Chamberlain
254 E.L. Wallis
255 Stone CE Combined School
256 Mrs N. Rose
257 Peter B. Dublin
258 Laurie Milner
259 R. Smith
260
262 Dr Ian Beckett
263 Bodleian Library
264 Public Record Office

Remaining names unlisted

ENDPAPERS: A remarkable photograph of the 1st Bucks Rifle Volunteers drawn up under the command of Lord Addington at Addington Park, 1893. Elements shown include the cyclists (left rear), the band (centre rear) and the ambulance wagon (right rear). (AMOT)